THE
DEATH
TRAIN

A Personal Account of
a Holocaust Survivor

THE

LUBA KRUGMAN GURDUS

DEATH
TRAIN

A Personal Account of a Holocaust Survivor

HOLOCAUST LIBRARY
NEW YORK

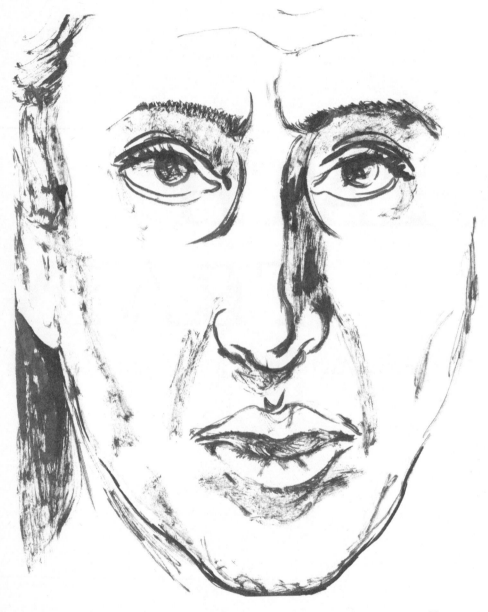

Self-portrait

IN MEMORY OF MY SON
ROBERT MICHAEL GURDUS
(1938–1942)
AND THE MILLION JEWISH CHILDREN
WHO PERISHED IN THE HOLOCAUST

JACKET & ILLUSTRATIONS BY THE AUTHOR

TYPOGRAPHY AND PRINTING BY WALDON PRESS, NEW YORK
MANUFACTURED IN THE UNITED STATES OF AMERICA

PREFACE

WORLD WAR II CAUGHT ME IN POLAND. Fighting to save my family and to stay alive, I was unable to compile a day-to-day diary, and whatever notes I was able to make, I later lost or destroyed. All I salvaged were my mental and visual impressions.

When the war ended, I began to draw from the reservoir of my private and precious bits of recollections and found that my experiences were entwined with feelings and emotions that I was still not ready to bring to light.

Time has passed, and I now feel a moral obligation to speak up. As one of the survivors of the indelible years of the Holocaust, I feel urged to speak up for myself and on behalf of those silenced by the Nazi oppressors and unable to reveal the web of deceit which paralyzed their will and judgment.

The "Final Solution" of the Jewish problem was a cold and calculated crime which must never be forgotten. Before World War II, the Jewish population of the world was estimated at about 16,000,000. About two-thirds were concentrated in eastern and south-eastern Europe, including just over 3,500,000 in Poland, which was clearly the home of the largest Jewish community of free Europe and the center of Jewish social, cultural and spiritual life.

During the World War II German occupation of Poland, the fate of the Jews was decided. On October 21, 1939, Reinhard Heydrich, chief of RSHA (Reichssicherheitshaupamt), instructed Adolf Eichmann to solve the Jewish problem. The German master plan for the "final solution" was put into effect shortly thereafter.

During the following years, the Jews of Poland were systematically isolated from the rest of the population and confined to ghettos and forced labor camps. In addition, Jews from nearly all occupied European countries were brought to Poland for annihilation.

By the end of World War II, the number of Jews murdered by the Nazis in Poland reached a staggering figure of 6,000,000. The German master plan proceeded in stages with such cunning that it was difficult to perceive what they ultimately had in mind. In their death drive, the Germans applied all means and methods to reduce the Jewish population through starvation, disease, degradation, dehumanization, and in the last stage, genocide.

In September of 1939, the first Jewish ghetto was created in Piotrkow. The Lodz ghetto was established in August 1940, and the Warsaw ghetto, in October of the same year. On October 13, 1940, Governor Hans Frank issued an official order which served as basis for the establishment of 500 Jewish ghettos in all of occupied Poland.

Gradually the small town ghettos were incorporated into the closely isolated ghettos of larger cities. In addition, forced labor camps were formed, among them Plaszow, Poniatowo and Trawniki.

The mass slaughtering of Jews began in the former eastern provinces of Poland in the early months of 1941. In December of the same year, the first Jewish extermination camp was established in Chelmno. During 1942, a complete destruction of ghettos was carried out in central Poland. In March of 1942, the Jews of Lublin were sent to Belzec, and in the summer of the same year, they were followed by the Jews from the entire Lublin district. We were among them. Under the pretext of "resettlement" the Nazis sent the Jews to the extermination camps in Belzec, Treblinka, Sobibor, Oswiecim and Maydanek.

The annihilation of the larger ghettos was more of a problem. The partial liquidation of the Warsaw ghetto started in July 1942. It was followed by a second assault on the ghetto in January 1943. In February, Himmler ordered the total destruction of the ghetto. The Jews retaliated with a mass uprising which lasted six weeks. The spirit of the Warsaw ghetto fighters, which arose from ultimate despair and defiance of death, has astonished the whole world.

The Warsaw Ghetto Uprising was not an isolated occurrence. The spirit of resistance was demonstrated by most of the Jewish communities. Fierce battles with the Germans occurred in Bialystok, Baranowicze, Kovno, Vilno, Cracow and Lodz. The Bialystok ghetto uprising occurred August 16–19, 1943. It resulted in the deportation of twenty thousand Jews to the camps of Poniatow, Blizyna, Maydanek and Oswiecim. Even during the liquidation of prisoners the Jews demonstrated collective resistance.

Officially the Germans exterminated the entire Jewish community of Poland, except for a negligible number of inmates locked in forced labor camps, and eventually freed by the Allies. In fact, however, about thirty five thousand Polish Jews survived the war, a mere one percent of the prewar population of Poland.

INTRODUCTION

HOW SHALL I WRITE an introduction to a story that defies its very narrative? I first met Luba Gurdus some thirty years ago. She came with her memories—vivid, stark and dark reminders—flashes from the past put down in black and white on paper. When she opened her portfolio of drawings—portrait of her life in a concentration camp—I was catapulted back to those brutal days of Nazi terror and bestiality.

Here stood this gentle, sensitive woman who came from the shadows of Hell. In her person, she symbolized the grace and dignity of the Jewish people who even at the threshold of death called forth the greatness of God and goodness of man.

Her drawings were incorporated in a special Holocaust issue of our Congress Monthly. Even after so many years and tears and books and paintings and films, her record of Holocaust life remains vivid before me.

And then there was the other face of Luba—her paintings of the hills of Jerusalem and the land of Israel.

I have often thought of Luba and her past. What courage it required to live in the camp; to survive without collapse at the loss of family and child. And to be reborn whole and good. She has faith in herself and love for humanity.

She rebuilt her life around this faith—that after evil—justice must follow as day follows night.

And now after three decades, she finds the strength and repose to relive the life she left behind. Her words and her drawings are conjoined to produce a volume of memoirs that is not only a notable addition to the library of Holocaust literature; it is a book that is a personal odyssey and an inspiration to all of us who may at times falter in our faith and in our belief that in our time and in our lives we witnessed the destruction of one world and the rebirth of a new world. And Luba has lived to tell this story and to be witness to this miracle.

JULIUS SCHATZ

ACKNOWLEDGEMENTS

S PECIAL GRATITUDE is extended to the National Council on Art in Jewish Life and, in particular, to Julius Schatz, Executive Secretary, for his advice and kind assistance which made possible the accomplishment of this task.

I am deeply indebted to my editor, Judith Sokoloff, and to Alexander and William Donat for their assistance in shaping this book.

Warm thanks are due to my family and friends for the encouragement during the period of work.

Above all I am grateful to my husband, Kuba (Jack), for his continuous concern and for his enthusiasm and support which were instrumental in bringing this book into reality.

Map of Poland

TABLE OF CONTENTS

TABLE OF ILLUSTRATIONS

CHAPTER ONE

THE SURRENDER OF WARSAW

M Y SON ROBERT MICHAEL was born in 1938 on a very warm August day. I remember the crowded waiting room at Vita Clinic in Warsaw and the young nurse who took me to the doctor's office. We had just arrived from Konstancin, where I spent the early summer months. In the picturesque garden surrounding our house I enjoyed many relaxing hours, painting and reading. That morning I had been putting a few finishing touches on the first of what I hoped would be a series of family portraits when mother became concerned and took me to the clinic.

Hours later I woke up with my son's first cry. He was suspended in the air, slim and brown as if tanned by the sun. His head was covered with shiny, black hair and his fingernails were pink.

"My little monkey," I whispered.

After the siege

"Monkey!" snapped back the young obstetrician. "This is the prettiest baby I have ever delivered."

The next thing I remember was the room, filled with flowers and my family. There was mother with her black hair forming a fine frame for her alabaster skin and gray eyes; and father, with his tanned complexion and bushy hair showing a bit silver gray at the temples. Their eyes reflected great joy.

The door opened and the nurse brought in the baby; the jubilant, young father jumped to his feet to look at the white bundle.

My husband was tall and slim. His broad shoulders and low neck supported a shapely head with a narrow face marked by strong features and enlivened by soft brown eyes. I had met Kuba in Warsaw where his family had settled after fleeing Russia in 1917. He was sent to a

5

As we descended the staircase

German high school and an American university and rejoined his family in the early 1930s.

Kuba took his son and placed him close to me. It was late afternoon and the sun was sending its last rays through the drawn curtains. One touched Bobus' nose and his little pink hands went into action. The family burst into laughter.

What happened, where did our happiness go?

One year later on a September morning, my son woke up early and opened his violet-blue eyes. He looked at the window and said in one breath: "The sun is out—let's go for a walk." This was his first sentence and I was alone to enjoy it.

It was September 1939, and the Germans were on the outskirts of Warsaw; the city was under siege. Kuba and my two brothers were gone, responding to the appeal of Polish military authorities, which urged all young men to abandon the city. So far we hadn't heard from them.

I dressed Bobus and fed him powdered milk. As we descended the staircase to the shelter a dull explosion disrupted the morning quiet. The house trembled, and a whiff of crisp air entered through a staircase window. I hurried down the last few steps. Another explosion sent a cloud of dust and loose stones from the rough shelter ceiling. The light flickered and darkness enveloped us.

The shelter was packed; a few people moved, making space near the entrance. Our neighbors discussed the food shortage while their children slept. The stench of unwashed bodies and children's discharge was suffocating. "Let's go," insisted Bobus. "Let's go, the sun is out."

I gave in. It was a perfect autumn day. When we reached the courtyard, a formation of German fighter bombers appeared in the pale blue sky and dropped a shower of white bundles. One fell near us. It contained a dozen leaflets calling for unconditional surrender. The delivery of propaganda concluded the morning bombardment.

The following few hours promised to be quiet. I took my son home, then headed to the river carrying two buckets. The streets were totally deserted and marked by the destruction left in the wake of the two week siege. I stumbled over stones, bricks, glass and broken powerlines, passing barricades made of piles of torn sand sacks and barbed wire. The ground was wet because of broken mains, and I slid along the mud trying to reach the only undamaged waterpump in the vicinity.

From a distance I saw a tightly crowded queue, which was longer than usual. I joined the line and observed the women waiting their turn impatiently, ready to disperse at the sound of an approaching plane. The numerous craters near the pump justified their concern. A day ago a German fighter had strafed, injuring several women. It took more than an hour to fill the buckets which were half-empty by the time I got home. After a few minutes rest I took off for the local distribution point for our daily bread rations.

The place was crowded with people cursing and fighting. Two soldiers tried to calm the excited throng in vain. An argument had arisen over two bearded Jews who were waiting to collect bread. An angry Pole attacked them, claiming they didn't belong to this distribution area and were depriving others of their share. I finally received my bread rations and rushed home. My baby was sound asleep; mother told me Bobus had refused to eat. She and father looked tired.

The prolonged siege triggered an intensified German attack on Warsaw. In addition to bombardment, the invaders decided to break the resistance of the population by systematically setting fires in every borough. At night the sky was aglow with flames, mounting from the crumbling houses.

The homeless inhabitants of Warsaw fled from one street to another. One night a score of homeless relatives including my sister-in-law Anne with her family and maid arrived at our house. Refugees flocked to the city from the suburbs, which had fallen into German hands, adding to the confusion. Warsaw was filled with desperate and hungry people—fear and apathy took over.

The belt around the city was tightening. German planes, dropping incendiary bombs, kept us on the watch day and night. Several of them fell on our house but were extinguished by a crew of tenants organized by father, who was always the first to lead the fire fighters. The situation became unbearable, and a general demand for a quick solution forced the city authorities to accept the German terms for unconditional surrender.

On September 26, 1939, the city capitulated. Two days later, Major General Tadeusz Kutrzeba signed the document of surrender. One of its foremost conditions specified that the Polish armed forces must relinquish all arms and leave the city.

It was still dark when the contingent of Polish soldiers stationed in our courtyard started to leave. Father, assisted by tenants, had supplied them with food during the siege, and now provided them with civilian clothing. They left one by one to avoid drawing the attention of the Germans who were already occupying the city.

On Sunday, October 1, the German army entered Warsaw, creating resentment and fear. The "triumphant entry" was well organized. The long column was headed by ambulances and field kitchens. Rows of military trucks followed, the last equipped with a movie camera. Uniformed soldiers of the 10th division—hardly showing any combat fatigue—marched at the end.

All day the triumphant army paraded to the beat of drums. "Boom, boom"—the deafening sounds were echoed by my pounding heart. The arrogant enemy kept on marching, mockingly celebrating the funeral of the city.

"One, two, one two . . ." How could I stand it? I ran to get away from the numbing spectacle. Circling, I took longer than ever to reach the house of my in-laws. The entrance to their courtyard was blocked by bricks and rubbish but the house was intact. The elevator was out of order, so I climbed to the eleventh floor.

Kuba's mother opened the door and greeted me joyfully. She took me by my hand to the living room where the family had gathered at the table. Kuba's parents had aged. Out of their eight children only Rosa and Genia, were present at the table. Gosia had left for the United States. Clara was in Palestine, Gucia in Latvia, Leon in France and Nathan, the youngest, probably in Rumania. Nathan, his whole life spent in a wheelchair, was the foreign correspondent of the London

The Family had gathered at the table

Daily Express; he had been evacuated by the British Embassy at the beginning of the war.

"Where is Kuba?" asked Genia.

"What will happen to us?" inquired my father-in-law.

There was no end to the questions. Problems were mounting and there was no apparent solution to any of them. I tried to console my in-laws but without conviction.

I left the house with a feeling of growing despair. My head was spinning but the cold of the evening put me on guard. The street looked unfamiliar, dark and scary, and I was afraid to walk slowly. Odd characters stood at the corners, and a German soldier passed with two girls; their giggling was accompanied by the curse of a crippled, old woman. A lonely dog barked in the ruins of a house, and a drunkard holding on to his bottle grumbled, "No lights, no sidewalks, what is it? One can break his neck in this rubbish." Holding my breath, I quickly overtook him and ran until I reached our house; the janitor assured me that everything was all right.

The next few days were filled with tension. Young men, who left Warsaw on September 6th at the request of the military authorities, started to filter in. Many were injured and told gruesome stories about their ordeals.

10

Days went by and we hadn't heard from our boys. Finally, one October morning they returned—unshaven, dirty, their jackets torn. Kuba entered the courtyard followed by my two brothers, Escha and Mela. Escha, the elder, was slim and dark. He had inherited father's olive complexion and mother's gray eyes, protected by generous framing. After high school, he studied business administration in Berlin but was forced to leave Germany in 1933. Mela, slightly taller and with a lighter complexion, was an athlete and member of the London University rowing team. He returned home for summer vacation with an injured leg and was still dragging it with great effort.

Several windows opened and friendly neighbors welcomed the boys. I left Bobus with mother and ran to greet them; it was good to have them back.

The reunion did not last. With the influx of returnees, the Nazis ordered all young Jews to register at collection centers from which they were sent to clean up the city and bury the victims of the bombardment. Displeased with the lack of response, they resorted to street arrests and a systematic house to house search for young Jews. Those who were caught were dispatched to forced labor camps.

Our boys remained in hiding. Kuba and Escha spent their time alternating between the attic and the cellar; Mela, completely disabled, stayed in bed with a physician's certificate under his pillow.

The situation of our young men became precarious. It was clear to them that they had no chance of survival under German rule. All looked hopeless when we heard that young Jews were massively escaping to the eastern part of Poland, occupied by the Russians.

We spent a sleepless night trying to persuade our parents to leave Warsaw. They refused to discuss the issue. Even Mira, the youngest in our family, was determined to stay in Warsaw and finish her high school studies, secretly conducted by her former teachers. She was tall and blond and could easily pass as Aryan.

The boys decided to depart immediately. "I prefer to die free than to live in slavery," stated Mela firmly. Kuba and Escha nodded in consent.

The next day, we learned that one of the tenants had crossed to the East several times and was organizing a group of Jews for his next trip. He already had enough people and was planning to leave the following morning. Our boys were ready to join. Kuba risked a quick visit to his family for a final good-bye and returned with his sister Rosa and her husband who were also anxious to leave. Without turning on lights, which could easily give us away, we stayed up all night. Shivering from cold and excitement, we spoke about our uncertain future and the prospects of seeing each other again.

Before daybreak the boys hurriedly dressed, each putting on two sets of clothing and sturdy boots. They filled their pockets with handkerchiefs, small sums of money and passports, hoping not to have to show them at the border. The bulk of the money had been given to their guide, Kazik, the only Gentile in the group. They were meeting him at dawn.

Kuba opened the nursery door quietly to have a last glance at the baby. He turned to me and whispered, "Are you ready to let me leave you alone with Bobus? Are you?" Without answering I hugged him and gave him a few photographs of the baby.

A thick fog hung over the courtyard. The boys crossed it singly with Kuba at the end. He stopped to wave for the last time—then he too disappeared behind the gate.

At midday, the persistent ringing of the doorbell interrupted our meager meal. A husky German entered the dining room and ordered father to follow him outside. I protested, causing the arrogant German to raise his voice and threaten to take me along. In the courtyard, father joined a group of elderly Jews guarded by a corporal who escorted them to the grounds of the Polish Parliament at Wiejska. I followed the group inconspicuously.

The men were met by a sergeant who reviewed the contingent with disdain. He evaluated the physical potential of the participants and divided them into two groups, assigning one to dig graves and the other to handle the corpses.

I found an opening in the fence which surrounded the grounds. Young Poles had gathered there to cheer the Germans who were abusing the old men. The ingrained Polish hatred of Jews had burst open.

Father, assigned to the group of grave-diggers, struggled with the heavy shovel, forcing it into the dry ground. He stopped momentarily to wipe his forehead. A fat German yelled at him, then resorted to his whip. The digging went on for hours without respite. Bored by the lack of excitement, the Poles gradually left. The fat German unexpectedly took father behind a bush, then to the gate.

Father was totally exhausted. His back hurt and his palms were covered with blisters. He was lucky the German had used an opportune moment to take his watch and discharge him.

12   After November 12, 1939, every Jew twelve years of age or older

Father stopped to wipe his forehead

was compelled to wear a white armband with a blue Star of David on his right arm. This singled out the Jews, making them easy prey for Germans and Poles. Soon groups of Polish youths stormed through the streets of Warsaw shouting anti-Jewish slogans. They robbed individual Jews and broke into Jewish stores. The Polish police did not intervene. The Germans photographed the violence, using the pictures in magazines and movies as evidence of Polish hatred toward Jews. The gangs were headed by delinquents and fanatics. One was led by a madwoman and became a regular plague in our neighborhood.

One morning mother was confronted by the gang. They attacked and knocked her down, leaving her unconscious in the street. Fortunately, a witness helped her to the house. She was bruised and shaken; her coat and bag were gone. Several days later the madwoman cornered me in the street and tried to abuse my baby.

My strolls to the park with Bobus came to an end. All parks were banned to Jews. They were also forbidden to ride on trolley cars and were ordered to walk only on the pavement and remove their hats before passing Germans.

Our troubles mounted. One day father was arrested and taken to prison. I went to seek help from the Jewish Community Center. A trolley car, marked with a yellow star and assigned to Jews only, took me there. The Center was besieged by people of all ages. A mob of mostly women with children blocked the entrance. The line continued to grow, as hardly anyone was admitted inside. It was common knowledge that the Center was highly ineffectual in providing relief for the swelling numbers of Jewish refugees, and ironically it became a useful tool in the hands of the Germans. Through its various channels the Center succeeded in reaching the Jewish community of Warsaw, burdening it with German demands for manpower, taxes, ransoms and penalities. Gradually, the Germans transformed the Jewish Community Council into the *Judenrat* (Council of Jews), which served them in the ghetto.

The woman waiting next to me hoped the Center would be able to get her temporary living quarters or help her find her relatives. She had been thrown out of her apartment at night with her elderly mother and three small children. Their begging for mercy did not move the Germans, who would not let them touch their belongings and hardly allowed them enough time to dress properly and take some food.

A baby cried and her young mother gave her a piece of sugar while telling us the sad story about her ailing parents and missing husband.

The Center was besieged

15

She had been at the Center several times but they were unable to trace him. Time dragged on, and it was announced that the Center was closing for the day.

A week had passed since father's arrest and we still hadn't heard from him. The arrest had occurred the morning after a Saturday raid on our apartment by the Nazis. That Saturday night, a constant ringing of the doorbell announced unexpected visitors. Luckily, before the Germans reached our apartment, one of the janitors warned us, and father left by the rear door. A German officer, accompanied by two soldiers and a civilian, seemed to be on a routine check. Through his official interpreter, he asked for the house owner and house records.

Checking out the members of our family, the interpreter noted that all the men were absent and made a nasty remark about escapees and traitors. The officer assigned each member of the group to a different room and the search began. He stayed in the dining room and watched me feed the baby. After a while he asked my son's age and mentioned that his youngest, about the same age, lived in Hamburg.

After an hour of aimless searching, turning the entire place upside down, the officer realized the expected riches were just not there. He was about to leave when one of the soldiers went to the kitchen for a quick check and spotted two locked cases in the niche. Questioned about them, mother explained they belonged to a tenant who had left Warsaw. The interpreter informed the officer that, according to the new German law, we should be punished for "secretly" keeping Jewish property. Not quite certain about the allegation, the officer shrugged his shoulders and ordered the party to leave.

Father returned home for the night. The next morning he was surprised by a soldier who had a warrant for his immediate arrest. Ignoring our pleas, the soldier refused to disclose where he had been ordered to take his prisoner.

There was nothing we could do and no one to whom we could turn for assistance. The Community Center refused to help, claiming it had no authority to intervene in such cases. Mother succumbed to heavy depression, and Bobus continually asked for his grandpa to whom he was very attached.

One day, without warning, father came home—thin and pale. During his recuperation he told us about his stay in prison. Most of the prisoners were Jews, arrested for minor offenses. Some were caught during curfew hours, others without armbands, and most, like father, had been arrested without a "legitimate" reason. The Jews were placed together with criminal offenders, including common thieves, extortionists and murderers.

The days in prison consisted of roll calls, meager meals and aimless hours of waiting for the interrogation. Inquiries were filled with provocations, insinuations, threats and blows. Father was asked daily for his money, jewelry and other valuables that might have been hidden. Ignoring threats of violence, he consistently repeated the truth: All his assets were tied up in his real estate, and the war had caught him with a small amount of money with which he had paid off his employees. The Germans were not convinced; the interrogations went on and on. Finally, tired of father's story, they released him under the condition that he raise a substantial ransom in due time. The sad fact was that father had no hope of ever being able to get the money.

During father's convalescence, another intrusion disrupted our life. One morning, a Nazi sergeant and a Polish railway employee burst into our kitchen brandishing revolvers, trying to terrorize us. Amazingly, they were not interested in our apartment but immediately demanded to be taken to our cellar. I offered to lead them there, but they insisted that only father should accompany them. Still quite weak, he tried to tell them we had already been subjected to an official search by the German authorities, and our valuables had been requisitioned. The intruders seemed to know about it, arousing my suspicion that they had inside information regarding our household.

Under strong pressure, father finally took them downstairs, and I alerted the janitors, who, with, other male tenants, went to the basement. The intruders, hearing male voices and heavy steps, developed cold feet and ran.

It was clear we had an informer in our home. I recalled that Maria, our maid, often bragged about her cousin who worked for the German railways. There was a strong possibility this cousin had arranged the morning intrusion and even participated in it himself. I shared my suspicion with father and he decided to have it out with Maria at once. After a few direct questions, she admitted her involvement and begged for forgiveness, but father, nevertheless, discharged her.

Acting like a trapped animal, Maria went to pack her belongings. Jumpy and nervous, she tried to avoid my inquisitive eyes. "Why did you do it to us, Maria?" I asked. There was no answer.

When I hired Maria, she was a widow and seemed grateful to have a home. I soon discovered she was lazy and mean and often fought with the baby's nurse. When the war broke out, Maria began acting   17 strangely. During the bombardment, she disappeared evenings and nights, always finding an excuse for her absence. She eventually admitted she had befriended a soldier stationed in our courtyard and was bringing him food and clothing, stolen from Kuba's wardrobe.

After the cease-fire, Maria continued to stay with us without salary. She was regularly visited by a "cousin" who would usually leave carrying bundles. I noticed that during these visits, Maria, pretending to fetch coal for the stove, would run down to the cellar, where we kept bottles of perfume left by a tenant. I tolerated her excesses patiently, until she actually endangered father's life.

Maria's sobbing was repulsive—I couldn't wait to see her go. To my surprise, she came back after a week, peddling food. I refused to see her, but mother, concerned about the acute shortage of dairy products, bought milk for the baby and encouraged Maria to supply it regularly. For a time she sold her products, smuggled in from a nearby farm. Then one day she came to tell us she was moving to the country.

In December, Wladek, a Pole formerly employed by father, arrived from the Russian occupied zone, bringing the first news from our boys. They were in Bialystok, staying with father's sister Sonia. According to Wladek, they were discouraged by the experience with their guide, Kazik, who abandoned them at the border between the zones. Only because of Escha's keen sense of direction did they find their way through the forest and avoid the Russian patrols. They walked for almost twelve hours before reaching Bialystok, and Mela arrived in a terrible condition.

Wladek thought the most logical thing for them to do would be to try to reach Lithuania, still unoccupied—a window to the free world.

"I wish they would do it soon," said father.

"I will repeat that," promised Wladek.

He told us that in the Russian Zone food was plentiful but expensive. Peasants did well, selling their produce at exorbitant prices. There were no jobs and money was scarce. People were spending it all on food, and even if they wanted to buy clothing, there was little available.

"If clothing is in demand," I said, "perhaps we can sell some and supply the boys with money?"

"Not a bad idea," nodded Wladek. "Give me a coat, perhaps a fur coat, if you still have one."

"Will mother's Persian be all right?"

"A Persian is fine—they'll appreciate that."

We had hardly any money in the house which could be sent to the boys, and I was afraid that the sale of a fur coat would not solve their problem. Something more substantial had to be done. Without giving it a second thought, I asked Wladek if he would take me along. "Of course," he answered. "But if you come, we have to move fast."

My parents were petrified, afraid to let me take the risk. "Why do you want to leave us?" asked father. "Without you we will be lost, and you may not be able to return."

Torn between the desire to help the boys and care for my parents, I said, "Why don't we all leave?"

"We are too old, and the baby is too small to risk the crossing," stated father. Mother did not intercede, but I knew her answer would have been yes.

Wladek took my passport and urged me to say good-bye. After kisses, hugs and tears, I was on my way. It was close to curfew hour; the streets were deserted. The cold air revived me, and I suddenly felt an influx of energy and a growing satisfaction from having made my decision.

The railway station was crowded. An unruly mob tried to push its way to the ticket window. It shocked me to see Poles in good spirits, even joking. What a long time it had been since I had seen a heartily smiling face.

A few railway employees tried to maintain order, but no one took them seriously. Even the police officer in attendance was mercilessly pushed around by impatient travelers. Wladek disappeared for a while and came back with two tickets.

"How did you get them?" I wondered.

"I have my ways, let's go."

The waiting room was packed. Most people slept in the dim light. A plain-clothes man sized up the new arrivals. As his cold, penetrating eyes fell on my fur coat, a sudden whistle diverted his attention, and the crowd surged to the exist. A sea of people pushed with determination towards the train. For a while I lost Wladek, who suddenly grabbed my arm and shoved me to the nearest steps.

The train was dark inside. All seats were occupied, and we stayed in the aisle which was also solidly packed with passengers. A German station master shouted: *"Los, los, einsteigen!"* (All aboard!) and the train pulled out. The darkness was comforting. Standing between Wladek and a husky peasant, I tried to relax and collect my thoughts. If everything worked, I might soon see Kuba and my brothers.

19

At the first stop several people left, vacating seats in a compartment with a broken window; a penetrating chill seeped in. The train stopped a few more times until only a family of three remained in our compartment. They seemed to be well-to-do Aryans from the city. The young boy was tall and blond, slightly resembling Kazik, the treacherous guide, who had probably taken advantage of many Jews, anxious to get out from under German terror.

Crossing the border was a frightening experience. I had heard about beatings and arrests by the Gestapo. While trying to evade the Germans, many Jews had fallen into the hands of the Russians, who confiscated their possessions and turned them back with a casual *Dawaj nazad* (Get back). Confronted with the growing influx of Jews from the German Zone, the Russians did their best to discourage illegal traffic.

Our trip was coming to an end as we approached the last stop in the German Zone. The dim lights of Malkinia appeared in the distance. Somewhere ahead was "no man's land," separating the two zones. Suddenly the train stopped; many doors opened and scores of young people jumped out into the dark countryside.

"This was obviously fixed," whispered Wladek.

"Why don't we take advantage of this?" I inquired anxiously.

"I never walk when I can still ride," answered Wladek.

The human shadows quickly disappeared in the field, and the train moved on. My eyes followed the last of the escapees with genuine envy; I sincerely wished I were among them.

It was almost midnight when the train finally reached Malkinia. The squeal of the train brakes was accompanied by the barking of dogs and shouting. *Los, los austeigen!* (All out!) bellowed the Germans who surrounded the train.

A few station lights illuminated their broad shoulders and shiny rifles. Eyes glued to the window, Wladek watched the Germans running along the platform. The train came to a final halt, and our car stopped opposite the platform exit, guarded by a sentry. Fortunately, the guard was not on duty, and we jumped through the exit, finding ourselves outside the station. A Polish railway employee gave us directions, pointing to the brightly lit Gestapo headquarters down the road.

We began to run, haunted by desperate voices coming from a distance. One voice came through clearly: "Jesus, Maria, have mercy, we are not Jews!" A thicket of bushes separated us from a clearing hemmed in by a dark forest on the opposite side. This was "no man's land," dividing the two zones.

It started to snow and the wide field was quickly covered by a white blanket. Wladek led the way, followed by three train passengers. Tired from the weight of the fur coat, I stayed at the very end. We almost made it through the clearing when a faint whisper in a mixture of Polish and Russian came from the forest: *Chodz, chodz siuda* (Come, come here). Wladek turned around instantly and ran back; I followed. A salvo of gunfire pierced the air just above our heads. Bending over, we ran to the nearest rock and hid behind it.

"I am glad you had the good sense to follow me," said Wladek, breathing heavily.

"I was lucky to be far enough from the forest."

"Now we have to wait," decided Wladek, carefully looking out from behind the rock.

The snow was still falling. I looked back at the undisturbed clearing from which our footsteps had already disappeared, and there was no sign of the three Poles or their Russian captors. It was quiet; but we were trapped between the bushes and the forest and there was nothing we could do except wait. After an hour the group of people who had left the train before its final stop approached us, asking for directions. Wladek advised them to cross the clearing at a distance from the forest. All went well.

It stopped snowing and the moon disappeared behind a thick cloud. We decided to move when a second group of people began the crossing. Wladek joined them and soon assumed the role of leader. I followed, stumbling over barbed wire, broken branches and snow-covered pits, always at a considerable distance from Wladek, who turned frequently to check on me. The march lasted for hours.

Every night "no man's land," between Malkinia and Szepetowka, was crossed by hundreds of Jews. Some were caught by Germans, others were turned back by Russians. Those who succeeded in eluding both enemies still had to contend with loose gangs of bandits who would offer to provide transportation and later rob them.

It was almost dawn when a few tall peasants in white sheets blocked our path. They offered us a ride in their horse wagons for a handsome sum. Older people soon filled the wagons, and although I would have gladly joined them, Wladek decided to continue on foot.

"We have only two hours to the station," he explained, "and I am not sure their intentions are good."

At six in the morning we reached Szepetowka, and as soon as we mounted the train, it moved out of the station. The trip to Bialystok took an hour.

I had left Bialystok after high school graduation and returned several times for short visits with the family. I was attached to the city and never stopped loving it. Looking at the dilapidated railway station and the shabbily dressed crowd, I saw that here too things had changed. Some familiar faces smiled at me. Jews here still smiled.

An old school friend approached me and asked about the family. I was too exhausted to talk. We hired a horse-drawn cab and moved on, bouncing on the old cobble stones. I thought about my childhood and adolescence. The bridge we crossed was our favorite hangout, and on the left was a warehouse complex which belonged to the family. Every turn revived more memories. A milk wagon passed and turned into the market place with its high clocktower.

The town was still asleep. Several Jews walked by—without white armbands. The policeman at the corner did not pay much attention to them or the passing cabs. We finally reached the house where I had spent the early part of my childhood. Within minutes I was upstairs greeting my paternal grandmother Zlata.

The commotion brought out the rest of the family: my aunt Sonia, her husband Abram and their daughter Rachel. They greeted me with tears in their eyes. Kuba and Mela stormed in and hugged me.

"How are you dearest, how is the baby?" asked Kuba.

"How was the crossing?" inquired Mela.

The door bell rang and Escha entered the room. Shocked to see me he exclaimed angrily: "What are you doing here? Didn't you know crossing the border between the German and Russian zones is punishable by three years in prison?" He showed me the front page of his morning paper with headlines about the new law.

"Calm down," interceded Kuba. "She is already here and not going back."

"What do you mean, she is not going back?" said grandmother. "She has to go back—she left the baby."

"I have to go back, I left the baby," I echoed grandmother's words.

"Let her rest," concluded Kuba, "and then we will discuss the matter."

I didn't feel tired. Excitement had killed my fatigue, and I could not afford to lose one precious minute of our reunion. I joined the family for a breakfast of fresh bread and salami. A samovar of steaming tea added to the festivities. The boys dug in with gusto; it was good to watch them eating and joking like old times. Considering our food problems, I asked about the local conditions.

"Food is no problem here so far," said Escha. But it is expensive and we are nearly penniless."

"Wladek told me about it—how did it happen?"

"It's very simple," said Mela. "We lost our money during the crossing—it was taken by our guide, Kazik."

"That scoundrel," I commented. "Wasn't he paid for the crossing?"

"Don't waste time talking about him," begged Kuba.

"Fortunately I have brought mother's fur coat and my jewelry so you can replenish your resources and move out of here."

The next day, a decree cancelling Polish currency and removing it from circulation in the Russian Zone made my "imports" doubly desirable, particularly because I was able to accept Polish Zlotys for them. Uncle Abram received a spectacular price for the fur coat and even more for the jewelry. A new spirit entered the house. The boys regained their energy and drive and started to plan a move toward Vilno, which was in the still unoccupied Lithuania.

We spent several days and long evenings discussing the possibility of escape into a country unoccupied by Germans. It was difficult to get used to the idea of another separation; we tried to delay the painful moment, but postponement was dangerous.

Early one morning the boys began preparing for the journey. This time there was not much to pack and not much to say. We all cried, feeling this separation might be final and that each of us was facing a difficult and uncertain future.

In the afternoon I went to see my maternal grandfather Berel. After grandmother's death, he lived with a housekeeper. Mother tried to induce him to stay with us in Warsaw, but he missed his home and synagogue and felt isolated in new surroundings. Grandfather's four sons lived in the United States, and they too had begged him to join them.

I found him at the kitchen table, munching a piece of bread and drinking milk. He had become thin and frail and stayed in the house, unlike his former self—the outdoorsman who loved his garden, cattle and dog. Grandfather invited me for a glass of milk and asked about my parents and son.

"I heard you crossed the border and hoped you would come to see me," he said. "Do you have a picture of your son?"

"No, I don't; but we will soon come to see you—the war will not last forever," I said reassuringly.

"But I am an old man, old and tired. When are you going back?"

"As soon as I hear the boys have reached Lithuania."

"Oh the boys," said grandpa, "I saw them once."

"They left unexpectedly," I tried to explain.

"I hope you will come again, but if not, just tell your mother that I miss her very, very much."

The following day I visited father's brother Meier. He used to live in a two story mansion, but the Russians had requisitioned his house and taken all his belongings. Uncle's family consisted of a wife and six children. One daughter, Luba, had emigrated to Palestine; three married daughters lived in Bialystok, and his only son disappeared after he was arrested by the Russians while crossing into Lithuania. The youngest daughter, Riva, who was my age, stayed with her father and stepmother. She told me about her vain efforts to secure a job. Ironically she had been turned down on account of her father's wealth, when, in fact she had to support him. Riva complained about her struggle and tried to impress me with the complexities of life in the Russian Zone. She did not realize how lucky she was to be on this side of the fence.

After a few more days in Bialystok, I finally received a message saying the boys had reached Vilno. This was a signal for me to leave. It was not easy to find a guide; the Russian three-year prison term for illegal crossing discouraged Jews and Poles alike. Luckily, a friend recommended a Polish girl who was planning a trip to the capital. Zenia had crossed the border several times and was ready to risk it again. Her attitude was reassuring.

The next morning we met at the station. Zenia had one arm in plaster to convince the Russians or Germans she was seeking medical attention in Warsaw. I was to pose as her traveling companion.

The train ride to Szepetowka went smoothly. A Russian border guard in a long sheepskin stopped us at the station, and pointing his rifle at us, shouted: "Where are you going?"

"Come along and you'll see" said Zenia resolutely. Shocked by the blunt answer, he shrugged his shoulders and left.

The usual route is heavily guarded," explained Zenia. "We have to make a circle, and this will take more time. Our first stop will be at a nearby village where I have to make a delivery," she continued, while inspecting the hilly countryside. She stopped abruptly and made a turn to the right, beckoning me to follow. I looked up and spotted a group of Russians coming down a nearby hill. "Hurry," urged Zenia, running along the path. About a dozen people passed along the main road walking straight toward the Russians.

"Shouldn't we alert them?" I asked.

"No, unless you want to share their lot. Remember," she added, looking around, "don't try to save the world, concentrate on yourself if you want to survive this mess."

Zenia stopped and knocked at the door of a small hut. "Praised be Jesus Christ," she greeted the surprised woman.

"Forever after," answered the woman, inviting us inside.

Her husband seemed to have doubts about us. The peasants had been warned by the local police not to house newcomers heading toward the frontier. The woman looked out of the window, and seeing the Russians entering the village, led us to an open barn where we stayed during the house-to-house search. When the patrol left, we abandoned our hide-out and advanced to the next stop up the hill, not far from where we had previously seen the Russians. Now there was no one in sight. We reached Zenia's friends' house within minutes. The barking of the dogs alerted the owners, and they asked us inside. The smell of food and freshly-baked bread invaded my nostrils. The peasants were busy with their elaborate preparations for Christmas Eve.

"What are you doing here on a holiday?" asked the stocky woman.

"I had no choice—I am on my way to see a medical specialist in Warsaw," explained Zenia, pointing to her bandaged arm. Flashing one or her irresistible smiles, she added: "We will stay here only until dark; can you give us a piece of your bread?"

The woman moved reluctantly to the oven and returned with a bit of steaming bread. "Here," she murmured, and ignoring Zenia's thanks, slammed the door behind her.

The afternoon dragged on. Hidden behind drawn curtains, I looked at the crisp snow caressed by the dazzling winter sun. Sharp blue shadows saturated by red sunrays turned to softer violet in spots. A cat, climbing the waterpipe, jumped onto the roof of a low farm building. The peasants disappeared into the barn, followed by their faithful dog.

The house was dark, and the smell of food simmering on the open stove was intoxicating. I closed my eyes and dozed off. The sharp barking of the dog and loud Russian voices came as a shock. We hid under the beds and waited.

"Who is hidden here today?" inquired the Russian.

"Today is Christmas and there is nobody here," giggled the woman. "But let me give you some fresh bread and ham." She hurriedly got the food for the Russians, who wished her a merry Christmas and left. It started to snow. The peasants came in and began to prepare for the evening meal. They watched us, visibly annoyed by our presence. Zenia promised to leave at dusk but asked for a white sheet, offering to pay for it. "Take it and go," implored the woman.

Covered by the white sheet, we moved slowly through the empty stretches of snow separating the two zones. There was no one patrolling; soldiers were probably celebrating Christmas Eve. Dim lights at the foot of the slope indicated the German Zone. We reached the first house on the outskirts of the village undisturbed. A tall man answered Zenia's knock.

"Blessed be Jesus Christ," said Zenia.

"Forever after," snapped back the man. "What do you want?"

"We are looking for lodging," answered Zenia.

"On Christmas?" barked the man and slammed the door.

We tried the house across the road. A tiny gray-haired woman appeared at the threshold.

"What a day to travel on! Come in, come in," she invited. Inside, Zenia told her about her bad arm and the trip to the specialist. The woman listened patiently and encouraged us to take off our coats. Then she introduced us to her family.

Gathered at the table, presided over by an old patriarch, were young and old participating in the festivities. The traditional Christmas celebration continued for hours, and various members of the family encouraged us to partake in the hearty meal. After supper, our hostess spread two mattresses on the hall floor and promised to wake us in time for the train.

At dawn, after a glass of milk and a slice of bread, our hosts took us to the station in their wagon. The village was asleep and the roads were empty. We had almost reached the station when a German patrol car appeared on the road and stopped us. The young officer instructed his interpreter to inquire about the purpose of our journey. Our driver, acting in good faith, pointed to Zenia's arm and explained the situation. The unconvinced German looked suspiciously at all of us but let us proceed.

A few minutes later the train to Warsaw arrived. It was almost empty, and the windows were covered with thick frost. An icy wind entered the compartments through broken window panes, badly mended with wood and paper. At each stop a few passengers, loaded with heavy bundles climbed the slippery steps.

A peasant, frozen after a long wait, entered our compartment. He dropped his pack and began hopping from foot to foot, rubbing his numb hands. Then he took out a small bottle of vodka and treated himself generously. After warming up, he passed the bottle around. He was smuggling an extra large load of food to Warsaw, hoping to make up for his last venture in which he had been caught by the Germans, who confiscated his food without reimbursement.

The peasant was right; the trip passed without an inspection— undoubtedly due to the holiday, which kept most travelers at home, including the railway police. Everything was also peaceful at the Warsaw railway station, though we had to wait for a horse-drawn cab and share it with other passengers.

The emaciated horse moved slowly through the snow-covered streets. The few passers-by included an old Jew, who hung a bag over his arm to conceal his armband.

After a long ride, the cab finally stopped at 13 Hoza Street. I entered our apartment through the rear door and found the entire family assembled in the kitchen. Father looked thin; his face had yellowed and acquired the transparency of parchment. Mother had aged, and even the baby looked smaller and paler.

"I knew you would be back, I knew it," said father with tears in his eyes.

"The boys are in Vilno" I whispered. "Now let me introduce Zenia, my guide and wonderful traveling companion."

After we entered my room, Zenia immediately removed the plaster which she had worn for the last 36 hours. Her arm was stiff, but there was no trace of injury, only a huge bundle of Polish money.

"So this was the dangerous infection which demanded the immediate attention of a specialist," I giggled. "Zeniczka, I am eternally grateful to you for taking me home."

"Any time, Luboczka. Would you like to go back with your parents and the baby?"

"Would I? But of course! Let me talk to father and maybe he will agree. If not right now, surely in the spring."

"Don't worry, we will think of something and find a way."

CHAPTER TWO

LEAVING WARSAW

T HE RAIN DRUMMED on the roof of the car as it moved along Hoza
Street. I watched the reflection of the faint yellow street lights in
the wet pavement. The car crossed Plac Trzech Krzyzy and
moved quickly to the outskirts of the town. Our driver was taking us to
a small village in the District of Lublin.

We had left our Warsaw apartment with Gentile friends, Colonel
and Mrs. J, who had arranged our passage to Brody Male, giving us
their car and driver. We were trying to avoid compulsory eviction to
the northern sector of the city, restricted to Jews only.

The inside of the car was dark and the air filled with excitement.
The driver remained outwardly calm and watchful, realizing the grav-
ity of the responsibility undertaken. He had planned the trip carefully
and was taking us through narrow and dark side streets, heading toward the last outpost on the outskirts of Warsaw. So far everything had
gone smoothly; and the heavy rainfall provided a protective shield. We

The gate to the Warsaw Ghetto

passed one policeman, and the sentry box was empty when we reached
the main road leading south to Lublin. The road was bumpy and
treacherous, but the driver continued with speed, and we settled in for
the long drive.

I looked at my family in the rear of the car. Bobus was fast asleep
in mother's lap; Mira slumbered, leaning against the back seat. Only
father was awake, tensely watching the road. It was good to relax in the
darkness of the car and get away as far as possible from the terrors of
Warsaw and the confinement of the ghetto.

On October 16, 1940, the Nazis had issued an official decree
establishing the Warsaw Ghetto. October 31 marked the deadline for
an exchange of the population. Within just two weeks, all Jews living
outside the ghetto area—about 150,000—had to move into its fatal
boundaries. And the 80,000 Gentiles living inside the ghetto had to
move out.

Prompted by the order, I went to the northern sector of the city to look for an apartment. I soon found out that however difficult it had been to move to the ghetto before the decree, it was certainly impossible to do so now because of the overwhelming number of people competing with each other for housing. The boundaries of the ghetto had been changed three times, and each time, previously assigned streets were carved away. Some of our friends, had moved several times. The last few days of October were chaotic. I saw Jewish families moving with their meager belongings. I saw young and old dragging, wheeling and carrying their bundles and crowding one another as they converged on the few official gates leading to the ghetto. No help of any kind was available. Pushcarts, about the only means of conveyance, were piled with household appliances, often confiscated without explanation by the Germans at the gates. The sad picture of the old and abandoned lingered in my mind and I shivered at the thought of my own helplessness . . .

I must have dozed off, and woke up when the driver made a sharp turn from the main road to an intersection leading to Lublin. A few military trucks emblazoned with huge swastikas passed. No private cars were on the road.

It was well after midnight when we reached the city. A few policemen were keeping watch over the rainy streets, but none left his shelter to stop us. The driver cautiously avoided the center, and after a complicated drive through a dark and totally deserted quarter, he approached the road leading to Szczebrzeszyn. When he slowed down at the bumpy crossing, the driver of a car across the road motioned us to stop.

A German soldier approached our driver and asked: "*Haben Sie einen Ersatzreifen?*" (Do you have a spare tire?)

"Sorry, not one," answered our driver.

"*Das is aber Pech!*" (This is bad luck!), murmured the German. We drove off. Dead silence in the car gave way to a whisper about the miraculous deliverance from danger. Our driver, shaken by the incident, remained silent. He was obviously relieved when we reached our final destination in Brody Male.

The settlement was asleep. There were no lights on in the long rows of houses framing the narrow road. At the end of the village was a group of taller buildings, including a well-lighted, two-story house. "This is it," said the driver.

The barking of the dogs brought out the owner of the house, who greeted us spontaneously: "Welcome, welcome, good to have you here." He was a husky man in his early forties, with a tanned face and white teeth glistening in his broad smile. "Please step inside. You certainly deserve a rest."

Leading the way, Mr.R opened the door to his house crowded with cheap furniture and numerous objects in utter disorder. Our host quickly removed a few items from the red velvet sofa and armchairs and encouraged us to make ourselves comfortable; after a few polite words he went upstairs to his quarters.

At dawn a sharp knock at the door got me on my feet. I grabbed my coat and looked through the half-frozen window. A German soldier paced the courtyard, examining the tire tracks in the snow. I opened the door and the soldier quickly approached me and asked in broken Polish: "What was the color of the car which left these tracks in the snow?"

"Black," I answered.

Not convinced, he looked around and spotted the owner's son in the shed. He repeated his question and received the same answer.

"I am looking for a green car," said the German and left.

The noise woke up the family. A few minutes later Mr.R appeared on the staircase landing, and flashing a smile, greeted us with a loud "good morning."

He took mother to the kitchen, which was as neglected as the rest of the house. Empty cans and beer bottles were scattered all over, and unwashed dishes were piled in the sink. Mr.R apologetically explained he was a widower, busy earning a living for his children—with no time for his household. He insisted we use his bread and milk, and after breakfast took us to his cousins' house next door.

"You probably know," said Mr.R, "that your friend, the colonel, has added a whole new room to my cousins' house for your stay in Brody Male. I hope you will find your new quarters comfortable and my cousins hospitable and civil."

The room was light and spacious, and our new hosts polite. Their ten-year old daughter Krysia smiled at Bobus, but Mrs.L's two brothers greeted us coolly.

Happy with our new surroundings, we unpacked our belongings. Bobus jumped around with unbounded energy and enjoyed looking out of the small windows which faced the courtyard and the main road. The four windows were adorned by new curtains, which gave the room an air of freshness and comfort.

"It seems almost unbelievable that we left Warsaw only yester-
day," said father. "I hope we will be happy here."

In the afternoon, father went to look at the sawmill across the
road. Against mother's advice, he wore his white armband with the
Star of David. A passing peasant looked at him with apparent curiosity
and amazement.

"It would have been better not to wear the armband," decided
mother.

"But what if they denounce us?" Mira asked.

"Wherever we turn, we are in a jam," mother concluded.

Father returned from the sawmill full of hope. He was elated by
Mr. R's high regard for his knowledge. Among the workmen were several Jews from Szczebrzeszyn, who looked up to father for guidance
and protection. Father was certain he could make himself useful in
many ways and contribute to the productivity of the sawmill, which so
far had not been much of an asset in the newly established Lumber
Mill Corporation, headed by Colonel J, our benefactor.

The company's head office was in Zwierzyniec. Adjoining it were
the quarters of Genia M, the colonel's sister-in-law. She promptly

Ghetto food hunters

visited us in Brody Male with an office employee, who was charged with providing us with food from the company's canteen. Our prospects brightened and our hosts, anxious to share the food supplies, became very friendly. We now believed our stay in Brody Male would work better than expected.

The first weeks passed in relative harmony. We enjoyed the change of pace and the good country air. Our peace of mind was, however, upset by the letters arriving from Warsaw.

We learned from our family that the Warsaw Ghetto had been closed November 15, 1940. On this fatal day the walls, raised by the Germans, were joined to form an enclosure reinforced by barbed wire.

The conditions inside the ghetto were terrible. The food situation, which had been serious from the start, became worse with every new transport of Jewish deportees from Germany, Austria and Czechoslovakia. And the severe winter had created a serious fuel shortage. People were cold and hungry; disease was rapidly spreading. Mira's friends who worked in hospitals wrote about epidemics and people dying from malnutrition, starvation, typhus and tuberculosis. So far our family had survived the difficult conditions, but their endurance 33

Starved . . .

was rapidly deteriorating. In spite of the tremendous risk, they contemplated secretly crossing to the Aryan sector of Warsaw even though some who had done it disappeared without a trace.

Compared with the news from Warsaw, our daily troubles seemed insignificant. We felt, however, that our placid existence in an all Polish village was built on a fragile foundation which could crumble any moment. Plagued by a feeling of insecurity, we hoped the German authorities would never force us to move to the ghettos of the neighboring small towns.

Life in these ghettos was trying. German extermination methods, applied in large cities, were well known to small-town Jews. A multitude of prohibitive rules and ordinances plagued their lives. Most of the young had been taken to labor camps, and those who were spared had a hard time surviving. They were forbidden to seek employment in the few local industries, trade with the peasants or leave the town limits without permits.

The Jewish Community locked in the ghetto was headed by the *Judenrat* and had to pay taxes imposed by the Germans. Misery among the Jews grew steadily and was aggravated by the Germans, who often invaded the ghetto to loot.

The widow Chana held an important place in the Szczebrzeszyn Ghetto, for she secretly kept a grain grinder. The local Jews depended on her resourcefulness for their bread, and the peasants, for grinding their surplus grain, which they hid from the Germans. Chana was assisted by her two grown daughters. Malka, the older daughter, baked the bread while Etla kept watch outside. Chana knew too well what to expect from the Germans for illegal grain grinding. Both she and Malka worked in a well-concealed cellar, known only to close friends. Also, Chana camouflaged her occupation by being known as a seamstress.

I met Etla at the corner where she told me her mother was at the sewing machine. I climbed the stairs, left my coat for repair, then went to see the cobbler across the street.

. . . And dying

35

The entire ghetto was crowded into a few streets not far from the river, which flooded regularly each spring and weakened the foundations of the wooden houses. The muddy puddles made the street difficult to cross. Jumping from stone to stone, I watched the emaciated Jewish children, who made the street their playground and amused themselves by sailing newspaper boats along the narrow gutter. A small boy sitting comfortably in a puddle threw a stone into the water, splashing my coat.

The cobbler's wife appeared in the doorway and greeted me with a faint smile, which twisted her toothless mouth. In a high-pitched voice she summoned home her youngest; little David crawled out of the mud and approached her, wiping his wet hands on her skirt. The woman took him upstairs, mounting the dilapidated staircase with effort. I followed her to a dark room furnished with a stove, table and a few iron beds. At the only window was the cobbler's bench, piled with shoes of all colors and sizes. At the sound of my voice, the cobbler raised his pale face with protruding, bespectacled eyes and greeted me apathetically.

36

The Szczebrzeszyn Ghetto

I gave him my new bundle and asked for father's shoes. The cobbler got up and hugged his son. David moved his chair to the table to watch his mother reach for a smoky pot and pour a watery substance into a chipped dish. Pushing it toward him, she encouraged the boy to eat; but after a spoonful, he pushed the plate aside and demanded a piece of bread.

"There is no bread in the house," said the woman apologetically.

"Give me bread, mother," demanded David.

The cobbler dusted father's shoes with his elbow and wrapped them in a newspaper. I paid, and he promptly handed the money over to his wife, who went to Chana to buy a loaf of bread.

At the corner I again passed Etla who inquired about a job for her younger brother at the sawmill. I promised to talk to father. Once outside the ghetto, I removed my armband and took a short cut through the fields. Still depressed by what I had seen, I did not appreciate the beauty before my eyes. The meadows on either side of the path were all in bloom. The crisp, spring air was impregnated with the aroma of early blossoms, which extended their delicate petals to touch 37

Bobus followed the movements of Mira's lips

the afternoon sun. It was peaceful and quiet with no one to disturb the beauty of nature.

When I reached the courtyard, Amor's barking brought me back to reality. The cows were eating from their troughs, surrounded by chickens busy picking the overflowing grain. Our hostess left the house with a steaming pot of potatoes for the pigs; her husband was unharnessing his horse while his father removed the wheat from the wagon.

I passed the busy courtyard and entered our room which was bathed in evening dusk. Mother was sewing, and Mira was reading Bobus one of his favorite stories while he rested his tiny hand on the book and intently followed the movements of her lips. I stood still, afraid to dispel the magic of the evening hour. Bobus raised his violet-blue eyes and smiled at me. A belated sunray lingered on his tiny head and jumped from one curl to another.

The next morning, a rumor spread throughout the village that there was an order from the German Military Command requesting lodgings for soldiers returning from the Yugoslav front. Their quartermaster arrived with his staff to requisition all available premises. He entered our house but did not find it suitable and left.

A week later, German soldiers arrived in Brody, and several of those lodged in neighboring houses became frequent visitors to Mrs. L's kitchen. She fraternized with them and fed them fresh milk and bread; they, in turn, gave her chocolate and cigarettes.

The presence of Germans in the village complicated our lives. Father stopped wearing his armband; but the Jews from Szczebrzeszyn working in the sawmill found themselves in a rather precarious situation. Afraid to move without armbands, they tried to be at work before dawn and return home after sunset. This added extensively to their working hours but kept them out of the Germans' sight. For a short time the scheme worked, until one of the Jews was spotted by a German who saw him enter the sawmill. An inquiry brought the German officer to the mill for an investigation. The owner tried to explain the need for Jewish workers and for father's expertise, but the obstinate German demanded that all Jews be immediately dismissed. And he insisted that father move out of Brody Male.

Father returned home, crushed by the verdict. He knew our relatively quiet days in the village had come to an end. The following day the German authorities ordered us to leave.

The sudden command came as a blow to us but hardly shocked or surprised our landlords. They did not offer any words of regret or consolation and seemed secretly pleased with the unexpected break, which enabled them to enlarge their living quarters. Only the sawmill owner was unhappy with the prospect of losing father's assistance. He offered to help with transportation and supply wooden boxes for packing.

At his advice we sent Mira to seek aid from the head office in Zwierzyniec, and she returned in the evening with news about temporary living quarters where we could move the following morning. The small flat, put at our disposal for a limited time, belonged to an office employee, who commuted between Warsaw and Zwierzyniec and would be away for a few weeks.

After a long night of packing, Mira and I got up at dawn and went to see our landlord to arrange our trip to Zwierzyniec. To our surprise he had already gone. We turned for help to our next door neighbor, a widow whose son, a theology student, was visiting during a holiday recess. The young man, sympathetic to our plight, offered his assistance. Without hesitation he harnessed his horses and loaded our belongings, ready to transport the entire family to Zwierzyniec. Mira and I decided to leave immediately and clean the flat before our parents' arrival, letting them follow in the coach promised by the sawmill owner.

The trip to Zwierzyniec went smoothly but took several hours, and it was close to nine o'clock when we pulled up in front of a dilapidated one-story building on the main street. A short woman opened the door to the flat and introduced herself. "I hope you will find the place comfortable," she said. "In case there is something you need, I'll be in my cottage at the end of the courtyard."

I entered the flat and looked around in disbelief. The walls and ceilings were cracked and marked with nests of tiny bug holes; the floors were chipped and warped from humidity, and the entire place, smelling musty, was in a state of disrepair. I opened the window and realized it was not much above the ground level.

"This place is really something," I said. "Wait till father sees it."

"I have already spoken to Genia about finding something else," answered Mira, "and I'm going to see her right now."

After some time the coach pulled up in front of the house. Father entered the flat, followed by Bobus. He looked around and said: "What a place—dirty, dark and cold like a grave." I gave him the only chair and made him relax. Mother came in with a few bundles and took them to the kitchen. Ignoring father's gloomy mood, she checked the kitchen stove and began unpacking her food basket.

It was almost dark when Mira stormed in through the door and proudly announced: "I found another place—light and clean; it's a little out of town but maybe that's better. Hurry, all of you, let's go there before it's dark."

"It will be impossible to transfer the luggage," I said. "Let me stay here with Bobus and you join me later, if you can."

Mira returned late. At dawn we were suddenly awakened by loud steps, husky German voices and a sharp knock at the door. Luckily our windows were tightly closed and protected by shutters, and the room was dark. A German peered through a crack in the shutter and tried to force the door. When he left we moved with our blankets to the windowless kitchen. The knocking continued, but we didn't budge, praying to God that it would not wake up Bobus, who could give us away.

Through a hole in the front door I saw a group of young Poles guarded by a German. When the raid came to an end, the young men and women were taken away, leaving their elders in the street. One woman cried desperately, trying to explain to a policeman who assisted the Germans that her children were needed for field work here—not in Germany. The policeman promised that the Germans would return for all those who escaped the raid.

After things had settled down, we risked joining our parents in their new flat. Afraid to attract the attention of our neighbors, we did not wear our armbands, which would protect us from the Germans, who were only looking for young Poles at the time.

It was exceptionally hot and muggy. We crossed the main street and took a short cut through the meadows. Bobus picked a few flowers for his grandparents. After a while, we found ourselves near the railroad tracks from which we saw a long row of small houses facing the fields.

"See the little house with the red roof?" asked Mira. "That's where they are." We entered the narrow path between the high wheat and emerged almost in front of the house. Mira opened the gate letting Bobus mount the steps with his bouquet.

The flat was bright and cheerful and had important advantages. Our landlady was a widow, who needed the income. She divided her house into two flats and rented one to two teachers who had a son about the same age as Bobus. Our apartment consisted of two rooms, both facing the fields, and was close to the head office and to Genia, who lived with her family just across the tracks.

The office continued to supply us with food from their canteen, and this was great help. Food was not easily obtained in Zwierzyniec, and the nearby market, guarded by the police, was banned to Jews. Each Tuesday, local farmers marketed their produce in the village, but the Jews were forced to acquire their food on the black market, which was tolerated by Polish police for a handsome bribe.

In order to keep a firm grip on illicit trading, the Germans issued an order forbidding Jews to use most of the accessible foods. White flour was a prohibited item; and during Passover, several Jewish families were heavily fined for the possession of white matzoh.

Most of the local Jews lived in deplorable conditions in the ghetto. Not unlike the Szczebrzeszyn Ghetto, this one was also confined to a few narrow streets, jammed with shabby houses to which the sun had little access. The Germans frequented the ghetto and robbed the Jews of anything they could trade for vodka in the tavern.

The local *Judenrat*, at the mercy of the Germans, was used as a means of exploiting the wealthier Jews of the community. Malka was one of them. She had a secret bakery and her handsome daughter Yentl delivered bread to customers outside the ghetto, even to the well-padded local police, who provided a shield for her clandestine distribution. For the last several days Yentl had not shown up, and I was forced to fetch the bread myself.

It was a hot day, and the ghetto seemed deserted. The men were at work and the women stayed indoors. A few, taking advantage of the dry heat, hung their wash outside; the children played hide-and-seek between the drying sheets. My arrival aroused their curiosity and an

41

older boy emerged from a narrow passage between the houses and tried to size me up.

"Where is Malka's house?" I inquired.

After a moment of hesitation, the boy pointed to a spacious building at the very end of the street. I knocked at the window, and Malka let me inside, apologizing for her sick daughter.

"Would you like to take your bread?" asked Malka.

"Yes, I would be glad to."

"Please be careful, and don't give me away," implored Malka, wrapping the bread.

"Don't worry, I'll be careful."

The hot summer of 1941 was followed by a cold and rainy fall. The days were short, and it felt good to stay indoors. When the rains gave way to snow, we became almost isolated in our little house.

Yentl, who was still making the rounds, supplied us with the news about the ghetto, where German visits became less frequent. However, the severe winter, combined with food shortages, caused an outbreak of typhus; Jews, denied medical attention and access to hospitals, died in hundreds.

All our hopes for survival collapsed in January 1942, when Adolf Hitler made it clear that, regardless of the outcome of the war, all Jews would be annihilated. The newspaper carrying Hitler's party anniversary speech was obtained by a Zwierzyniec Jew employed by the Ger-

Bad news

mans and secretly passed around. It became evident that we were doomed; the question remained—when and how?

The severe winter continued without a let-up. The heavy snow blanket extended from under our windows over the wide fields and up to the dark forest resting under a leaden sky. Even the tracks, rarely disturbed by trains running between Lublin and Lwow, were covered with snow.

One train made an unexpected stop in Zwierzyniec, and a woman was taken to the police station. She was under suspicion of being Jewish which she stubbornly denied, and refused to see a member of the local *Judenrat*. The Germans kept her in prison for a few days and then ordered her execution. During the ensuing weeks other similar cases pointed clearly to intensified German terror.

With the arrival of spring, the winter apathy was broken by a zealous planning for escape. The young hoped to join the partisan groups concentrated in nearby forests. The question was what to do with the older people and children.

Tension mounted when the new reports concerning German atrocities were instinctively linked to the freight trains, which began to appear on the tracks and run south to an unknown destination. These strange-looking trains were heavily loaded. Their tightly-sealed cars were slowly dragged along the tracks by over-worked engines, whistling, puffing and leaving behind a trail of black smoke with fiery sparks. Sometimes at night we were forced out of bed by the noise of these trains, which pressed on creaking wheels and caused the earth to tremble.

One night I hid behind a roadpost to look at a passing train. Not unexpectedly, I spotted several SS men in green uniforms in the first, brightly lit passenger car, which was coupled to the engine. The following freight cars, some with barred windows, were dark and crammed with men, women and children. I attracted the attention of some prisoners, but their voices were muted by the chugging of the engine and jolting of the wheels.

One woman threw out a scrap of paper attached to a piece of wood. I picked it up and read the few words addressed to a Lublin relative: "We are being deported, please save our children."

The following morning I took the note to Malka, whose brother, assigned to a painting job at the railway station, had promised to probe into the mystery of the freight trains. Adler returned home with shattering news.

43

Due to an official German decree, thousands of Lublin Jews were marked for forced resettlement. They were assembled at specially created collection centers and transported to the south. A railway employee, commuting between Lublin and Lwow, told Adler that at these centers he had seen Jews being escorted by Ukrainian guards to boxcars and pushed into them by the hundreds. In the upheaval families were separated, and mothers lost their children. Protests, screams and cries were ignored and silenced with shots. The overcrowded trains were dispatched to an unknown destination and at their final stop switched to a new spur where the Polish crew was replaced by Germans.

When the spring sun had melted the rest of the snow on the steel-blue tracks, long freight trains began crossing them day and night. The trains, longer than before, consisted of shabby box cars, which rarely had a barred window. While they were passing, I tried to count the cars and multiply the sum by the number of people inside. Each passing train left behind bits of paper, scattered along the tracks. They contained messages, warnings and farewells. One read: "Run as far as you can; we are going to a certain death."

One morning, Yentl brought sensational news about a boy who had escaped from a concentration camp and was hiding in the ghetto.

The camp was located just outside Belzec on the road from Lublin to Lwow and was bordered by swamps, quagmires and electric wires.

Mendel's story was sad. About a month ago he was caught by surprise and taken with his entire family to a collection center outside town. They camped in the fields with a crowd of people of all ages, guarded by Polish police and Ukrainians, who mercilessly shot anyone attempting an escape. At dawn they were jammed into box cars. Standing on his swollen feet, he spent days on the train, mostly dozing, only to be awakened by sudden stops. During one stop, some Ukrainians mounted their car and removed wedding bands from the women's fingers.

The air inside the train was stifling and the stench unbearable. People relieved themselves right where they were; and children, dropped by their mothers, remained in the slime and excrement. Some people took poison.

Finally the train stopped and was surrounded by Germans, assisted by a group of inmates. The prisoners were unloaded and divided by sex. They were told to undress and fold their belongings into bundles with their shoes tied together. Then they were lined up for selection. Mendel and a few other young men were separated from the group. All others were sent to the bathhouse.

They camped in the fields 45

From the surviving inmates, he learned that after the shower the prisoners were given imitation coffee and taken to an electrified disinfection hall where their wet bodies absorbed the strong current. The coffee was supposed to dampen the impact of sudden death; but neither the current nor the coffee were fully effective in stifling the screams of the tortured which penetrated to the outside.

Screams of the tortured . . .

. . . From the "disinfection" hall

Mendel, spared for a prisoners brigade that handled new arrivals to the camp, gathered up all his energy and escaped to warn others about the mass murder.

We finally had an eyewitness account of what was happening to the thousands of deportees passing Zwierzyniec. All speculations regarding compulsory labor camps ceased. The young became frantic, wanting to join partisans in nearby forests. Some decided to contact the Polish underground and secure faked papers. The old were desperate and uncertain about what to do.

In the meantime, the General District Command for the Province of Zamosc, anxious to control the restlessness which prevailed among small town Jews, spread a rumor about a newly-devised program, which would supposedly protect all Jewish participants. All Judenrats throughout the district were ordered to prepare detailed lists of Jews, stating their age, sex and profession. The Zwierzyniec *Judenrat* conformed to the Nazi order, hoping that all "usefull" Jews and their families would be spared from deportation.

Once again the Germans cunningly diverted our attention from pending doom and directed it toward immediate survival. Only the freight trains, passing daily, remained a persistent reminder, hammering it into our weary heads that the end was inescapable and the German promises, false and deceiving.

We must do something, I told myself with every passing train, but daily worries killed all initiative.

In the spring the Forestry Administration of Zwierzyniec was authorized by the Germans to employ Jews. The *Judenrat*, in charge of compiling limited lists of applicants, selected them primarily from their own families. All positions were quickly filled. These circumstances brought about a power struggle between the *Judenrat* and those excluded.

The rejected applicants turned for assistance to the Forestry Administration, which appointed father as their representative and charged him with the responsibility of organizing the Jews into an orderly task force. Father was deeply grateful for the assignment and decided to take the Jews to work the next day. In order to assist him I had to leave Bobus with Genia for the day and hoped he would be glad to play with her little daughter Bozenka. My son strongly objected to being dressed at dawn and refused his milk. I wrapped him in a shawl and walked across the field.

48   It was cold and wet. Genia's household was still asleep, but the

barking of the dog alerted the cook. I left my crying baby with her and rushed off to the assembly point.

Crossing the quiet village, I spotted the bent figures of my parents, walking at a slow pace. Mira was far ahead with a group of younger people. An official from the Forestry Administration, accompanied by a forester, joined father for a short conference and outlined the scope of his assignment. After the official left, father compiled a list of participants and divided them into two groups. One, consisting of young women assigned to planting trees, left with the forester. The older group, primarily married couples with children, remained to clear the forest.

After a short rest father took us to the dense forest for our first assignment. Walking along the narrow path, I looked at the tall trees coming alive under the rising sun; the forest was filled with a delightful assortment of pale spring colors and a vast symphony of voices. Frogs croaked playfully in deep ditches, and birds twittered joyfully as they hopped from branch to branch.

We passed the forester's white cottage, hidden behind lilac trees. His wife, with infant in arms, watched us with interest and quieted her barking dogs with a firm, "Shut up you devils—let the poor people pass."

The road wound around a small lake surrounded by pine trees. We passed the lake and entered a clearing covered with broken branches and debris. "This is where we stay," announced father.

The group stopped. Several women took their children to the forest and spread a few blankets on the ground for the youngest. Father divided the workers into small groups. Each was assigned to a section of the forest and supervised by a foreman who directed the gathering of the branches, which fed the fire in the center of the clearing. Tongues of crackling fire spurted into the air. We moved in the haze created by the dense smoke, but the work proceeded swiftly. By noon almost half of the job was done.

"We should be finished with the entire job by five," said father.

"What's the hurry?" the women asked.

"Don't worry," father reassured them. "There is plenty of work in the forest for tomorrow and many more days."

At noon father called for a break. Most of the workers retired to the forest to eat, rest and attend to the children. After the break father, pleased with the initial result, expressed confidence in his people. Aware of their limited capabilities, he was careful with his preliminary assessment of yield. Now he was sure they would be able to meet the demands of the Administration. When the forester arrived for inspection by late afternoon, the clearing job was finished.

"Good job, in fact too good," stated the forester with a touch of irony in his voice. "Why have all the needles been stacked away?" he asked, looking around.

"They are here," answered father, "and will be evenly scattered after the fires are extinguished."

"Very well then, see you tomorrow," nodded the forester.

It was dark when we reached the village. Mira rushed ahead to chop wood and start the stove; I brought in two buckets of water and peeled the potatoes. Mother arrived and took over the cooking to give me a chance to fetch Bobus.

When I entered Genia's house, Bobus jumped at me with joy, asking, "Mami, mami, where were you, why did you leave me alone all day?"

"I was at work, darling."

"Where were grandma and auntie?" pressed Bobus.

"We all worked, darling, we all did," I tried to explain.

Genia accompanied me to the door and whispered," Bobus cried all day and asked for you." I hugged my little darling and all my worries vanished. We hurried home and met our next door neighbor.

"Tell me please," I asked, "did the train pass at noon?"

"Yes, it did," she answered.

At night the rumbling of the train woke me up. I rushed to the door and found it wide open, with father watching the dark monster, which had only one brightly illuminated car window behind the locomotive.

"It's a real Cyclops," I said.

"I can't hear you," replied father.

Our voices were drowned out by the clatter of the wheels and the penetrating whistle of the engine. The train was of gigantic proportions and its load stupendous. I counted sixty two cars. Father was breathing heavily, and his temples were moist with sweat. He wiped his forehead and opened his shirt.

"Please, close your shirt," I implored. "It's bitterly cold." He did not hear; his eyes were fixed on the train.

A few windows opened. Our Gentile neighbors were awakened by the noise. The train passed, leaving behind a cloud of smoke. Windows were closing when one harsh voice came through loudly: "Those damned Jews—they won't even let one sleep at night."

Back in bed I thought about the events of the last few weeks. At the end of March the Nazis demanded a contingent of the remaining Jews for work at the Klemensow airport. Their increased military activity on the Eastern Front was also marked by a wave of terror and an accelerated resettlement program. On March 26th, about 2,000 Jews were forcibly evacuated from Izbica and taken by freight trains to Belzec. Several days later, an almost equal number of Czechoslovakian Jews were settled in their place. A similar reshuffling process was applied in Chelm and Zamosc, from where more than 2,500 were deported, and many were killed to make room for German and Belgian Jews.

All the small villages around Zamosc were thrown into a state of panic. We now expected the worst but did not know what to do. Rumors circulated that Jews were fleeing the ghettos and hiding in the countryside, forests and cemeteries. Some of the young joined the partisans; others tried to escape by train to larger cities. But all this was made nearly impossible by the hostile attitude of the Poles, who denounced the escapees. Many were subsequently arrested by the police and executed by the Germans.

Desperate Jews tried to raise money by selling their belongings, but most of them, unable to sell, simply distributed their possessions to Aryans. I saw peasants leaving the ghetto with loaded horse-drawn wagons and carts. Yentl told me that some Jews had built hide-outs in the ghetto and offered exorbitant sums to peasants to hide their children. Only very few Poles, tempted by money, dared to defy Nazi threats of arrest and death.

The atmosphere of uncertainty and danger was in the air even at work. Forestry, not considered *kriegswichtig* (war essential) did not protect us from deportation. The Forestry Administration was not interested in the Jewish problem and temporarily used cheap Jewsih labor at their convenience. It also had its own share of troubles, being blamed by the Nazis for its inability to control the partisans, who roamed the forests and sabotaged German war installations.

The window framed a blue dawn when father entered the kitchen with a lighted candle casting shadows on the white-washed walls. He started the stove and prepared tea while mother fixed the bread, covering it sparingly with marmalade.

In the forest, father had found his crew reduced by all the younger

51

men who had been rounded up for forced labor. Their wives were unable to concentrate on the job and worried about their old and young left in the ghetto.

The day was bright but our mood was gloomy. During the noon recess, Wagner, a member of the *Judenrat*, brought food for his daughters, along with exciting news about the death train—the *Judenzug* (Jew train) had been withdrawn for disinfection.

"Does this mean the deportations are temporarily suspended?" someone asked.

"This is what we hope," answered Wagner.

It was hard to believe. For a while we stood in silence, mourning

those gone. Then the group spontaneously gathered together, crying, laughing and hugging each other.

On April 15, 1942, the death train passed without the usual load and without the Gestapo escort. For days we asked ourselves what had caused the deportations to stop suddenly. Nothing made sense.

On Sunday the sun rose high and with it our hope for survival. Everything seemed better, and even the bitter coffee was tastier. At noon the church bells rang. I looked out of the window and saw our neighbors returning from morning prayers. Romek led the way. He left his parents and knocked at our door, asking to play with Bobus.

"Resettlement"

CHAPTER THREE

THE ZAMOYSKI PRINCIPALITY

BOUT THE MIDDLE OF MAY most of the Jews under father's supervision were discharged. Only a small group of young girls were kept to plant trees. At father's request some of the Polish girls were sent to instruct us. We lined up in two parallel rows so that each of us had a partner to watch. In the beginning the Polish girls moved slowly, giving us a chance to observe their skill. Then, apparently not accustomed to the slow pace, they raced through the rows, making it impossible for us to follow.

The work was tedious and our equipment, old and rusty. The forester, irritated by the heat, was constantly chiding us and criticizing our slow work. At noon, exhausted and discouraged, we retired to the shade and ate our food, hardly talking. The Polish girls went deep into the forest, and soon their husky voices filled the air with cascades of laughter.

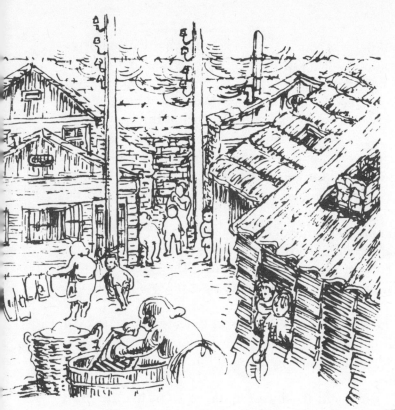

The Zwierzyniec Ghetto

At four o'clock the Polish group left. We were still working when Prince Marek arrived on his motorcycle to check the planting. Tall and slim, with a monocle in his left eye, he was the true image of a Polish aristocrat, a member of the Zamoyski family—owners of the Zamosc Principality. Walking slowly between the beds, he shook his head in disapproval.

"This negligence cannot be tolerated," he stated, pointing at the inaccuracies left by the Polish girls.

"But these rows were planted by the girls who came to instruct us," protested father.

The prince, displeased with the remark, moved to the other row and summed up his assessment in one word: "Horrible."

"We did our best," said father, but his voice was drowned out by the roar of the departing motorcycle.

The tedious planting was soon over, and the Forestry Administration had exhausted almost all its projects. The only one left was the elimination of a wildly-growing, young forest, which caused concern. Under normal circumstances, such an undertaking would be rather costly and risky. Cheap labor gave the Administration the opportunity to try.

The forest grew in a swamp. At the site several Poles worked on a drainage system, which would divert the excessive moisture. In order to make the system more effective part of the forest had to be cut down.

Father was again put in charge of hiring a large crew, but this time came up with a small group of mostly middle-aged men and women. They accepted the job reluctantly, only because they were eager to remain under official protection should there be a renewal of deportations.

The next day, the forester waited for us at the site to discuss with father the method of using the labor force. The men were assigned to tree cutting, and the women and grown children to trimming and stacking the branches.

The job was difficult, and the forester stayed to watch the progress. The young man showed a personal interest in us, and was curious about what had brought us to Zwierzyniec. He revealed that he also had been forced to escape from Silesia in order to avoid his responsibility as *Volksdeutsch* (ethnic German). In a sudden gesture of sympathy he offered me his small Canadian ax, which was exceptionally well-suited for trimming branches. The ax was very sharp and could be handled effectively with relatively little effort.

The forester became a daily visitor to the site, sensing that most of the crew were discouraged by the demands of the job. The ground, saturated with water, created unhealthy conditions which soon affected the undernourished and exhausted men and women. The road to the site led through several swamps and quagmires, difficult to pass and only partly covered by planks and timber. Most of the women had a hard time avoiding puddles and stumbled on the slimy ground. In addition, they were bothered by the Poles who amused themselves by removing the planks from under the women's feet.

Going home a more serious hazard awaited us at the fringes of the forest where German patrols showed up sporadically. They usually stopped us to check our working papers and take our belongings, even if they consisted only of a few vegetables bought from the forester's wife or a bottle of milk for the baby. On one occasion the milk was hidden in father's side pocket, but the German made a personal search and found it. After this, we hid the bottle among the cut branches we carried home.

The last obstacle before reaching the house were young shepherds, who herded cattle on meadows bordering on the forest. They tried to scare us by snapping their long whips at our feet. One day I snatched the whip out of the leader's hand—this stopped him.

At dusk we reached the blind alley leading to the house. A group of children played outside. Among them was Bobus who ran toward us calling, laughing and waving his tiny hands. Father grabbed his grandson, hugged him and carried him home.

Grandparents with grandson

The following morning only I accompanied father to the forest. Mira went to inquire about a new job, planning to join us later. The Canadian ax had gradually proved too hard on my skin, and I had to cover my bruised hands with old gloves. Nevertheless, I was determined to accomplish what usually was done by the two of us.

Next to me worked the three pretty Wagner girls whose father was a relatively wealthy man. Though raised in a small village, they had never done any manual labor and had a hard time dragging the wet branches.

But not Chana. The brave widow, assisted by her son, tried to spare the child, doing most of the work herself. She saw me dragging a heavy branch and offered to help. I assured her that Mira was due shortly.

Minutes later Mira appeared in the distance, and jumping from plank to plank, waved excitedly, shouting: "We have the job! The farm superintendent was reluctant, but Prince Jan, who happened to pass by, ordered him to employ us at the farm."

We were happy and so was father. We returned home in good spirits. This was an unexpected break. The forest job was coming to an end, and we had been worried about losing our employment papers. Mother urged us to take a break between the jobs, but Mira felt she had to keep her promise and report to work in the morning.

The next day father went alone to the forest, while we decided to go to the farm. On our way we walked through the small forest on the outskirts of the village. Emerging from it, we faced the county hospital, bordered by a French prisoners camp; the rows of white-washed barracks were hidden behind thick shrubbery and barbed wire. Further down was the Catholic cemetery with orderly lines of beautifully kept graves, surrounded by an elaborate wrought iron fence. It was peaceful and idyllic. Walking along the fence, I couldn't help comparing it with the mass graves into which thousands of Jews were dumped daily.

This is our fate, I thought—this is what we get for giving the world Jesus Christ with the love and compassion he had. The Romans tortured us in hundreds, and the Germans continue the tradition in hundreds of thousands.

My thoughts were interrupted by the farm bell. It was late and we had to walk faster. Dew still covered the grass along the path that led through wheat fields to the top of the hill, where a row of linden trees sheltered white farm houses with red shingle roofs.

The farm workers were all present and the superintendent introduced us. Accompanied by curious glances, we joined the column and started out for the beet fields, which spread like a thick green blanket on both sides of the steep road.

At the site, the foreman gave us new hoes and explained the nature of the job, which required cutting weeds around the beets without damaging their roots. We lined up, each girl facing her own field bed, and started cutting. The farm girls worked with ease, hardly touching the ground. Familiar with handling the hoe, used for tree planting, we followed the foreman's instructions, trying to imitate them.

The job was demanding and the farm girls' speed impossible to keep up with. Mira and I had to crawl on our knees with no time to turn around or even raise our heads. The foreman often gave us useful hints, and the girls watched us with curiosity. At the end of the day we were totally exhausted. The girls left almost immediately while we collected the waste, consisting of cut and damaged beets, hoping to trade them for milk for the baby.

It was after seven o'clock when we emerged from the forest. Afraid of Germans, we removed our armbands. Instead, we were confronted by the shepherd boys and our next-door neighbor. He pointed at us, yelling, "Look boys, these Jewesses live next to us!" Incited by the remark, the leader cracked his whip at our feet and the boys laughed.

The work in the farm lasted through June. On the first Saturday in July, we went back there to spray nitrogen on the small beet plants, which needed special attention. The farm girls were off, but the foreman came to assist us. The fertilizer was strong; it burned our skin and clung to our garments. We finished the job, and when the farm bell sounded at twelve, we were already on our way home.

On Monday, we learned that shortly after we had left the farm, the Nazis raided the fields. They were searching for partisans who had escaped after robbing the furniture factory. During the pursuit, a woman resting in the fields was hurt. It could have been one of us.

At the end of July we were sent home for the summer recess. A feeling of insecurity took hold of us again. The summer was exceptionally hot, and a renewed epidemic of typhus broke out in the district. Posters showing an old Jew as carrier of the disease were pasted all over the village.

In order to isolate the Jews from the rest of the population, the Nazis sealed off all the ghettos in the district and imposed severe penalties on trespassers, usually killing them on sight. With the news about restrictions came terrifying reports from Turobin and Szcze-brzeszyn, where hundred of Jews had been forcibly herded into the market place and killed by armed Gestapo men in public executions. The possessions of the executed were distributed among the Poles.

Terror had fallen upon the Jews of Zwierzyniec. They begged for employment, deluding themselves that this would protect them from deportation. Father was again asked to secure an assignment from the Forestry Administration and employ as many Jews as possible. With more eagerness than ever, entire families were getting up at dawn and leaving the ghetto for the forest; only the old and very young stayed behind.

One August morning the Germans raided the ghetto and took the few men they found. Among them were the two local shoemakers. Their mother begged the Nazis for mercy but they would not listen. After they left, the Polish police inspector called her, conveying a message from the Nazis; they decided to spare one of her sons—magnanimously allowing her to make the choice. The bewildered woman went home in despair. She returned in the evening begging for the life of the younger son.

Several days later the Nazis came back and arrested two members of the *Judenrat*, sending them to Bilgoraj as hostages. They demanded a substantial ransom for their lives, and though the money was delivered, the two men did not return.

The Jews now held nightly vigils in the ghetto and left a few older children to keep watch during the day. Among the children entrusted with the responsiblity was little Etla, a particularly bright child. Alert and courageous, she was sent by her parents to Zamosc. Hidden by a farmer among his potato sacks, she arrived safely at her grandparents' home. After her visit she was left without transportation, but did not hesitate to walk alone all the way back.

Seeing the Germans search the ghetto for new scapegoats, Etla decided to alert her parents in the forest. Her news stirred the Jews into panic. Confused and terrified, they were unable to make a decision. Some chose to remain in the forest; others, particularly mothers of young children left in the ghetto, returned to the village. On our way back we met the head forester who told us the Germans had left.

It was harvest time and the village was deserted. The local peasants were busy with their crops. Across from our windows, an old peasant was reaping his wheat with a long scythe. He was flanked on each side by his sons, who were in turn assisted by their womenfolk, who tied the cut wheat into bundles and piled them in big stacks in the center of the field. Most passers-by wished them luck.

Mother, unaware of the news, looked out of the window, and Bobus played outside with the children. A beggar with a sack suspended over his shoulder appeared on the road. The children interrupted their game and greeted him with shouts, "Jew, dirty Jew, go away." Romeczek approached Bobus and whispered into his ear, and Januszek, our landlady's eight-year-old, began to throw stones at the old man. Pointing at the beggar, Bobus turned to his grandmother, asking, "Is it true the Jew hides small children in his sack?"

"It is definitely not true," answered mother. "The poor man keeps his bread in the sack."

A shade of doubt passed over my child's face. "But granny," he tried again, "Romeczek said so and Januszek too."

Before sundown the death train suddenly appeared on the tracks. Young and old stopped to look at the monster with its multitude of box cars.

Januszek climbed the fence and pointing at the train said to Bobus, "You will soon be in a train like that."

"No, I will not," protested Bobus. "I won't go, I won't—you hear me?" he repeated, crying.

I walked out and grabbed my son who was trembling with sobs.

"Mother," he cried, "is it true?"

"No, no, it's not true my darling," I cried with him. "Janusz is small and stupid; we will not go, I promise you."

I grabbed my son . . .

CHAPTER FOUR

DEPORTATIONS—THE "DEATH TRAIN"

ON AUGUST 8, Mira came home trembling.

"What happened?" asked mother.

"Everything," she said. "Tomorrow is the deportation, and all Jews must report to the market place at eight o'clock in the morning with their employment papers and not more than ten kilos of baggage per family. The county chief's order came from Bilgoraj, and the *Judenrat* is responsible for its execution. A messenger is carrying the order from house to house and should be here soon."

I didn't believe it. The nightmare had suddenly turned into reality. Minutes later we saw the order, which summoned all Jews without exception to report for "resettlement." The messenger explained that the local *Arbeitsamt* (Labor Office) had decided to claim all factory and sawmill employees and was confident that they would be excluded from deportation. There was no hope, he thought, for Jews employed by the Forests and Farms Administration in view of the approaching fall and winter.

Collection Center for the District of Bilgoraj

After he left, I decided, nevertheless, to seek the aid of the farm superintendent. It was pouring. Stumbling through mud and slush, I couldn't help repeating, "This is the end, this is the end." Tears ran down my cheeks, my wet hair hung in strings. "Look at her, look at the Jewess," laughed the children. "She talks to herself—she must be crazy."

I finally reached the superintendent and told him about the deportation. He maintained there was no need for alarm and promised to intervene, but there was no conviction in his voice. Disappointed and worried, I went to the *Arbeitsamt* to see if employment with the Administration of Farms and Forests didn't indeed carry any weight. To my dismay, the *Arbeitsamt* didn't even have the Administration's list of Jewish employees.

Crushed by the discovery, I decided to pursue the matter and clarify it with the Superintendent of Forestry in the Zamoyski Principality. Mr. P, father's business acquaintance, received me cordially. He had already heard about the deportation and was surprised at my discovery. When he declared himself ready to accompany me to the *Arbeitsamt*, his wife interceded and advised me to forget about official intervention and escape. I asked her where I could go with my old parents and child, but she didn't answer. I left with the superintendent's solemn promise to have the list of all Jewish employees at the *Arbeitsamt* before eight in the morning.

It was clear that father's efforts to protect the Jews of Zwierzyniec had been turned into a mockery. They had been shamelessly exploited by the Administration and treated with total neglect. Now we were at the mercy of the Nazis and there was no one around who sincerely wanted to help us.

Rushing home, I decided to exhaust our last chance. I crossed the field and found Genia feeding her baby daughter. Sensing trouble, she asked the reason for my late visit. I told her about the deportation and explained the purpose of my visit. She listened impassionately to my request and answered without hesitation, "I am sorry but I have my own children to protect." Pretending not to grasp the conclusiveness of her blunt answer, I tried to explain that a small child like Bobus could hardly incriminate her. But Genia was not moved and pointed out that the sex of the child prevented her from even trying.

I felt the ground cave in under me. At my wit's end, I remained silent for what seemed an eternity. In desperation, I finally turned to her with my last argument. "In the name of God, then maybe Mira— maybe you can help her and send her to one of the colonel's offices outside Zwierzyniec?"

Genia remained silent. Seeing I was ready to leave, she muttered with apparent effort, "Let me think, I cannot make hasty decisions."

I crossed the field and met Mira at the gate. Afraid to look at each other we entered the house in silence and found mother busy in the kitchen and father playing with Bobus. They sized up the situation and tried to console us. "Please do not despair, children," said father. "Things may change. In the meantime, sit and eat in peace and don't worry—above all don't worry about us. Mother and I are reconciled to our fate."

Unable to answer, we sat at the table, feeling this might be our "last supper" with our loved ones. A sudden knock at the door interrupted the silence. Mira opened the door for Genia, followed by a stranger. "This is Zygmunt," she said. "He will take care of Mira temporarily until we can find something permanent for her."

Mother turned pale, unable to hide her emotion. Father, taken by surprise, hesitated for a moment, but took hold of himself and encouraged Mira to go.

My sister did not budge. Genia, nervous and agitated, tried to make conversation. Only Zygmunt remained calm and waited patiently until Mira finally pulled out a small bag and gathered some of her belongings. Without uttering a single word, she kissed each one of us and hugged her darling Bobus. When she started for the door, mother passed the baby to me and jumped to embrace her, breaking into sobs. Mira succeeded in quieting her, then turned for a final glance at us and disappeared behind the door.

The farewell

Unable to face each other, we retired for the night. After a short slumber I woke up. The events of the day and the deportation facing us were more than I could take. All along I had hoped this would never happen—that a miracle would save us at the last moment. But no miracle was in sight except for Mira's chance. It was comforting not to have to worry about her and to hope that at least she would survive the war and possibly meet our boys and tell them about us.

The kitchen was dark except for the silvery moonlight which stopped at the child's crib. I heard my parents whispering and entered their bedroom. Mother was crying and father, leaning against a pillow, tried to quiet her. He turned to me and spoke with effort:

"We are grateful to you my child that in these difficult hours you are with us. At the same time, I feel guilty having encouraged you to stay and having given you the illusion of being able to get you and Bobus through the war. Believe me, I never thought for a second we would be exposed to such cruelty and madness. The Germans I have known were different . . ." He paused. "I was afraid to let you run with an infant and had only your child's welfare at heart. Now all is lost and we are facing this terrible deportation. I have no illusions. This is certain death, and I would do anything to save you both." Father's voice broke.

After a while he spoke again: "As for us, we are resigned to our fate. We have always wished to go together, and this is how it will be. Death is a salvation for us; our faith is gone and so is our strength. It would be painful to survive and learn that our families, friends, indeed all Jews, had perished. I only wish I could see my two sons and Kuba once more." Father paused again.

"All our life," he resumed, "mother and I tried to do the right thing and did not falter in the face of adversity. We have toiled and raised a family with love and care, and now one fanatic madman has decided to destroy it all, to destroy all Jews. The world remains silent, and not a single, significant voice has protested this outrage. Where is the conscience of the world?"

Father's voice broke again. I checked his heart. It was racing and his temples were covered with cold sweat. I sat near him caressing his beautiful hands. Then he continued asserting his unlimited love for us and his unshakable trust in final justice. Finally, totally exhausted, he fell asleep. I left him and approached mother. Her face was wet; we kissed and huddled together, unable to speak. When she too fell asleep, I got up quietly and returned to the kitchen.

It was getting late, and there were still things to do before the fatal deportation. I took out a big sack and began packing—the child's warm clothing, warm underwear, socks, shawls, a wrap, a pillow, a few kitchen utensils, and on the very top, our documents. The sack was overflowing, but there were still many things we might need for the trip and our destination.

The packing woke up Bobus. He extended his tiny arms, expecting me to carry him to mother. Seeing me dressed, he asked, "Where are you going, Lolus?"

"Come, let's get dressed," I said. "We may soon have to go for a walk."

"But it's still dark," he objected.

Mother entered the kitchen and took the child. Father followed her and seeing me packed, asked, "Do you really think we should report to the market?"

"I packed just in case," I answered, "but I think we should see what happens and not hurry; maybe they will forget us and leave us alone."

The morning dragged on endlessly. After ten o'clock, a peasant returning from the market told me that quite a few Jewish families had reported with their bundles and were waiting for the Germans. Among them were government employees, painters, carpenters and tailors whose working papers had been approved by the *Arbeitsamt*.

Later in the day the Germans sent away all those whose services were vital to their war effort but kept the others and posted sentries around the ghetto.

The situation was dangerous. The remaining patrols indicated deportation was in progress. I was ready to go to the *Arbeitsamt* to check whether the lists of the Jewish farm and forest workers had been received from the Administration, but father would not let me move.

The early afternoon passed peacefully, and nothing indicated that the Germans were still rounding up Jews. Father looked out the window, and Bobus played outside. I was helping mother in the kitchen when a sharp knock at the door announced an unexpected visitor. A Polish policeman appeared at the threshold and asked me, "You are Jewish, aren't you?"

"Yes, I am, what about it?"

"And whose boys are playing outside?" inquired the policeman.

Bobus and Januszek entered the kitchen. The policeman turned to them and repeated the question. Before I had a chance to answer,   67

Januszek yelled, "Not I, I am not a Jew," and disappeared out the door.

I showed the policeman our working papers. He inspected them superficially and explained that the Forestry Administration had decided to keep only their factory and sawmill employees and that the others would not be excluded from deportation. He added, however, that it was not up to him to decide; he had to follow instructions to bring us to the police station. There was no way to make him change his mind.

Mother took the pot of boiling soup off the stove and extinguished the fire. The policeman advised her to take the soup along. Father, with his raincoat over his arm, waited outside. I dressed Bobus and threw the bundle I had prepared over my shoulder.

A group of curious neighbors assembled outside, among them our next door neighbor who took my keys. I raised my head and met a few sympathetic glances and a few grins. Nothing upset me, nothing bothered me; I was completely detached from reality. I walked, talked and adjusted my son's coat, but all I felt was an overwhelming desire to find a way to save my family from deportation. We walked slowly; mother, slightly bent, led Bobus by the hand; father, leaning heavily on his cane, held my arm. We passed the market place, watched by an ever-growing crowd of local Poles, loudly commenting about the event.

As we approached the police station, I saw a group of Jews being watched by sentries. I asked the policeman to take me to his chief, but he brushed me off and ordered the guard to take us inside. Father was pushed into a prison cell for men, and we were taken to a cell for women.

The guard opened a heavy iron door to a dark cell with one barred window. He pushed us inside and tried to close the door quickly behind us to escape pleas, cries and laments coming from within. The women begged for water and food for their children, but the guard ignored them and slammed the door.

A few women moved to make room for us on the stone floor. The children looked curiously at Bobus in his spotless blue coat and white sandals. Our nearest neighbor looked at the jar and asked about our food supply. Mother answered politely and sat on the bundle but Bobus refused to join her. He looked around and whispered to me: "Let's go home, Lolus."

The cell was jammed. The younger women gathered on the upper
level, and their children blocked the air from the only window making

In prison

the place unbearably hot. The lower level was dark and there the children slept. Bobus refused to sit or sleep, repeating persistently "Let's go home—let's go home—you promised."

I was getting restless and climbed to the upper level. It was still midday. Across the street, Poles strolled in their Sunday best, indifferent to the tragedy behind the prison walls. Their children played joyfully among the trees leading to the nearby park. A young Pole entered the police station. He looked familiar. Maybe he is from the Forestry Administration and has come to intervene for us, I thought. Another hour passed and nothing happened. Mother sat motionless, leaning against the damp prison wall. Bobus succumbed to a light sleep. The cell was suffocating—the guard had stopped emptying the overflowing pail.

I joined Father

A sudden turn of key in the lock alerted me. The guard opened the door and pushed a small dark girl inside. Behind him was an elderly Pole, who apparently had brought the girl to prison.

The girl stood at the door until a relative took her inside. She told us the girl's parents had been killed earlier that day, and they had left the child behind, hoping their Gentile neighbors would keep her. The girl's situation triggered a wave of remarks about how Poles were afraid to even try to save a Jewish child. Loud voices and spasmodic cries woke the children who joined in the lament, turning the place into an inferno.

Suddenly, loud German voices brought an instant halt to the weeping. The commotion outside, accompanied by a turning of keys, unmistakably pointed to the beginning deportation.

"Los, los, raus" (Move, move, out), yelled the Germans. The guard opened the door and ordered everybody into the courtyard. He

watched me reach for my bag, suggesting I leave it in his care. While his attention was focused on the bag, an SS man, annoyed by the delay, shouted at us in anger, *"Los, los, was ist denn da?"* (Move, move, what's going on there?) In German, I apologized for the delay and took the opportunity to tell him about our working papers. The Nazi brushed me off impatiently but promised to bring the matter to the attention of his superiors.

A large wagon, drawn by a skinny horse, entered the courtyard. The Polish policemen ordered all old women to mount the wagon. Mother was in the group and took Bobus along. I joined father, and we were included in a hastily formed column which was moved out into the street. "Look at their efficiency," commented father. "Their zeal deserves a better cause."

The wagon moved and we followed. After the dark prison cell, the street looked bright. It was full of curious onlookers who came to watch the unique spectacle. They lined both sides of the pavement and looked at the sorry procession. The emaciated horse, unable to cope with the heavy load, was slow; but the retinue of Jews were even slower. The head of the column consisted of old men and women with their children. There were few younger men in the column, which was solidly flanked on both sides by Polish policemen and the SS.

We crossed the market place, leaving the onlookers behind. On the edge of the road father spotted the watchman from the Forestry Administration. He moved to the end of the row and threw the surprised watchman his raincoat. The man caught it and waved excitedly, ready to throw it back.

"Why did you do it, father?" I asked.

"I don't need it anymore."

We moved slowly over the broken, sharp cobble stones, which hurt our tired feet and ruined our cheap shoes. The SS men, annoyed by the slow pace, urged we make haste, shouting and cursing. Soon father and I found ourselves at the head of the column. In front of us extended an almost unreal looking landscape illuminated by a flaming sun, which slowly sunk behind the dark forest, touching us with its fading glow.

The Germans sauntered along the column, guns swinging from their shoulders. They urged us on, promising a good rest at the collection center, and shouted intermittently, *"Los, los, ihr geht arbeiten!"* (Move, move, you are going to work!) "To work, to work," mimicked the Polish policemen, bursting into laughter.

71

The waning sun drenched the pale landscape with a last gleam of red. The marchers' muffled whispers mixed with the shuffle of their feet. The road ran along a forest with dense shrubbery. I felt a thousand eyes watching us from behind the bushes; eyes of sons and daughters following their parents being led to death, eyes of partisans waiting for darkness and an opportune moment to attack the convoy. My head was spinning with wild ideas of a miraculous rescue. I was unable to accept reality.

Marching at an even pace, father spoke again: "Look around you, look at these people. I feel sorry for them. They have spent their lives in misery and now they are forcibly led to death. Misery was their way of life. They lived alienated in hostile surroundings and were never

We walked in silence

treated as equals. Tolerated only because of their skills and resourcefulness, they were never loved or respected by their Gentile neighbors. Persecuted in many ways, they fought for their existence and succeeded in surviving and raising their children under the most trying conditions. They strongly believed their suffering would be rewarded by the ultimate triumph of goodness—and look what has happened.

"It seems that in every generation some Gentiles have risen up against us and devised a way to annihilate us, and the generation under Hitler has surpassed everything.

"Look, look at these people, meekly carrying the pitiful remnants of their lifetime possessions, still hoping they are going to earn their right to live through hard work . . ."

Father paused, breathing heavily, and resumed after a while. "As for us, mother and I have seen enough misery and persecution in our lifetime. We feel relieved in a way that this hopeless struggle for survival had finally come to an end. We are only sorry for you, my child and for Bobus . . ." Father's voice broke and a few tears came down his tired face. We walked for a time in silence; then father concluded in a voice swollen with emotion: "My only wish before I die is that my children should survive the war. I have no other wish."

"Father, please show your papers—they are still valid. You must try to survive and rescue Bobus; Mira will join you. I'll stay with mother to the end; they will not separate us."

"Don't ask the impossible. Let me leave this inferno."

"Father, this is all temporary. The Germans will soon capitulate, and you will take Bobus to Palestine and begin a new life with your grandson."

"It is too late for me. I cannot think about a new life without mother, even in Palestine. Life is hard there; the world does not care what happens to Jews anywhere."

"Hopefully people will start to care when they learn about the atrocities wreaked upon us. Our duty is to survive and awaken the conscience of the world for all future generations of Jews, particularly in Palestine."

"Who will listen to you, my child?" argued father.

A voice from behind interrupted our discussion. "Please dear, please help us," begged a woman surrounded by children, the youngest in her arms.

"Do not worry," said father, "everything will be all right."

"With God's help," added the woman.

The constant thought of approaching doom was becoming unbearable. I checked my working papers and looked for the SS man who was supposed to take me to his superior. He was at the end of the column. I did not burden father with my anxiety. His strength was failing, and he was leaning heavily on my arm. At a distance was mother holding Bobus.

It became dark, and the Germans, assisted by the police, closed in on us. The wagon rolled across the road ditch, onto a huge field overflowing with groups of Jews collected from the entire district. With bags, sacks and bundles—standing and sitting—they were crowded together and watched by Polish and Ukrainian guards. This was the collection center for the district of Bilgoraj.

When we entered the field, I spotted a group of Nazi officials dressed in striking green uniforms. They towered over the crowd, supervising the entire operation. The SS sentry who escorted us reported to his superiors. After a short exchange, he pointed at us and returned to take us to the officers. A young captain left the group and met us halfway. He asked father for his documents. Father handed over his working papers and explained he was employed by the Forestry Administration. The officer nodded and turned to me: "And you, what is your relationship to this man?"

"I am his daughter."

"What is your occupation?"

"I work at Wywloczka, a farm in the Zamoyski Principality."

The officer checked my document and said without hesitation: "Go, both of you, you are free."

Before I fully realized the meaning of his words, I saw another officer heading toward us.

"What is the problem?" questioned the approaching major.

"They have working papers," the young captain answered.

"Let me see them."

Father handed over his document. The major examined it carefully and stated: "This man works in the forest."

"That's right, he works in the forest, but for the sawmill," said the captain.

"And where does she work?"

"On a farm."

"Who needs farm workers in the winter?"

The captain, seemingly annoyed, gave up and was ready to leave. In desperation, I decided to appeal to the major. "During my studies in Berlin," I said, "I met many Germans and made many friends; why are you so inhuman?" The major amazed by my audacity, asked sarcastically, "And where in Berlin did you study?"

"At the Reimannschule," I said, recognizing him as a student from the workshop of Professor Hertwig.

"Reimannschule?" he wondered. "Which workshop did you attend?"

"I studied with Professors Hertwig, Gadau, Melzer, Schmidt-Caroll."

The major, obviously amused, turned to the captain and said mockingly, *"Schau mal, schau mal, das waere also meine Kollegin"* (Look, look, this was supposedly my colleague).

75

"Hertwig," he said, looking at me closely, "quite possible; you are certainly lucky. Go and take your father along."

When we started out the captain whispered to me: "Go quickly before he changes his mind."

"With our family?" I asked.

"Yes, yes, but without delay."

The Nazis rejoined their group, and we rushed to get mother and Bobus, who stood by the empty wagon. Mother looked at us in disbelief, and tears rolled down her face. She hugged me and whispered, "Thank God, thank God."

By the empty wagon

In a daze, I passed the sea of people and threw a last glance at the group of Jews from Zwierzyniec. There was the young shoemaker with his mother; the butcher's pregnant wife with her five children; little Etla with her parents; the dark woman from Warsaw whose son visited us daily to collect a pot of soup, and many, many others—all close together, looking at us with tears in their eyes. At the edge of the field, one of a group of Poles watching the deportation said jokingly: "You have just won a million!" Father unable to answer, pointed at me.

We left the field and took the side path in the forest. A long black car passed. In the front sat the Superintendent of Forestry, heading toward the collection center. "Late, but hopefully not too late," commented father.

I suddenly realized that I was in such hurry to leave the center that I forgot about the people who had asked me for assistance. I told mother I wanted to return. She looked at me in dismay. "How will you help them?" she asked. "After what I saw, the Nazis may even change their mind and keep you. The Superintendent will help them."

"But mother," I tried to argue, "he will only claim his employees, and will not bother about the dentist and her little son; she is a professional and should have been excluded from the deportation, but the police were too zealous, as with us."

"The dentist is a mature and intelligent woman and will speak for herself," interceded father putting an end to our argument.

We walked silently along the narrow path, followed by German shouts, which rose above the cries of the children. The sound of quick steps and crackling branches came from behind. I turned and recognized the tall, blond girl from prison. Krysia reached us completely out of breath and uttered between sobs: "The Germans let me go . . . a policeman explained that my father was a Gentile and had served with him on the force . . . but they kept my mother . . ." I embraced her gently and we walked together.

A policeman on a bicycle stopped. It was the one who had taken us to prison. He apologized remorsefully and told us that most of our belongings had been requisitioned by the municipality. The local officials were about to take everything, but Genia protested and claimed the furniture as office property. The policeman urged me to hurry, as the municipal building was about to close.

I took Krysia along and reached the village in minutes. On the outskirts, late strollers were still discussing the events. They looked at us suspiciously but did not stop us. We passed the deserted market place and looked through the broken gates at the main street of the ghetto. It was strewn with shattered glass, smashed furniture, torn bedding and broken dishes. Open windows and doors, moved by the wind made strange noises. A door slammed. "Who's there?" asked Krysia. There was no answer, and her voice returned in a loud echo. "It's the wind," she decided.

The municipal building was closed. I was drained of energy and wished to be home. We crossed the main street and entered the blind alley leading to our house. An open truck, overflowing with furniture, was being loaded by two office employees. Genia, accompanied by her older children, supervised the loading. She saw me coming and greeted me with surprise: "What happened? What happened to the family?" I told her they were returning. The men were ordered to unload the truck. A few curious faces appeared in open windows.

I entered the house and found it in a state of complete disarray. The whitewashed walls, stripped of photographs, were full of holes and looked dirtier than before. A few torn books were scattered on the floor, and a broken jar had been shoved into a corner. The closet was empty. In the kitchen I stepped on the photograph of our boys, sent from Japan. Here too the walls were marked by spots from where watercolors had been removed. On the floor, Janusz and Romek were busy dividing the books and toys belonging to my son. They looked at me and started to put them down. Voices outside announced the arrival of my parents and Bobus, who ran up the steps and entered the kitchen. The children greeted him with joyous surprise.

"How did you escape?" Janusz asked.

"Did the Germans let you go?" questioned Romek.

"Yes, Lola asked them to let us go," announced Bobus proudly.

"Have the car," said Romek, reaching into his bundle.

"Have the trumpet," followed Janusz, pulling it from his sack. The children started to play.

Genia sent her men home and stayed with us for a while. She wanted to know all about our release, and father tried hard to satisfy her curiosity. Our neighbor opened the doors connecting the flats and returned a few jars of marmalade she had taken before the arrival of the municpal officials. She added a loaf of bread.

Late at night, the Superintendent of Forestry, returning from the collection center, came to inform father about his successful rescue of all forest workers. Alerted by the Administration watchman who saw us leave Zwierzyniec, he drove to the collection center. The Germans were reluctant to grant his request because his list had not been officially approved by the *Arbeitsamt*, but finally gave in. When father was mentioned, one of the Germans recalled he had already been freed. The Superintendent thanked us for alerting him and helping him to rescue his employees. He seemed genuinely gratified by the outcome.

Long after midnight I entered the kitchen and found Krysia turning violently in her sleep and repeating, "Mother—mother." I covered her and went to bed.

At dawn a faint knock at the door woke us up.

"It's your mother," I murmured half-asleep.

Krysia jumped out of bed and opened the door. A jubilant outcry confirmed my guess. She returned to the kitchen with a tall woman,

Forcing the crowd into box cars

"Death Train" window

carrying a child in her arms. "This is my mother," she said, beaming with joy.

The woman put down the child who was clutching a piece of dry bread in her tiny fist, and embraced her daughter; they both wept.

After a while, Krysia's mother told us about her daring escape from the center: "When Krysia left, I spotted this lonely child and decided to escape with her. I moved gradually to the darkest corner of the field and found myself far from the crowd. Meanwhile, the guards tightened the ring, pushing the crowd toward the box cars. The uproar was tremendous. The younger men and women refused to move. The enraged Nazis increased their pressure on the Polish police and ordered them to use force, setting an example by delivering heavy blows to the most obstinate. In the upheaval, a few children, led by Etla, escaped to the forest. The Germans saw them running and sent their dogs in pursuit.

"I was well out of the Germans' sight when a policeman grabbed me by my arm. It was Stasiek, my late husband's best friend. He made certain no one saw us and let me go. Followed by wild shouts, gun shots and calls for help, I ran as fast as I could from this hell on earth.

Krysia's Mother

"*Los, loss*, yelled the mad Nazis. *Los, loss*, echoed the forest. I felt the earth tremble under my feet and the little girl cling to my back. I prayed to God to let me find you."

Mother and daughter embraced.

It was still too early to go to the municipal building, but I could not wait to redeem our belongings. Father advised me to stay home and not antagonize the greedy officials, but I was stubborn and left.

As I walked I thought about father's warning. He was at times too careful and wary. During the confiscation of furs from the Jews, he was determined not to hide anything and even included the child's calf coat. Ironically, the Germans questioned the number of furs received and accused the local Jews of sabotaging their order. They imposed a fine on the community, threatening to shoot four members of the *Judenrat*. In order to pay the fine, the *Judenrat* started a collection to

82

Children escaping into the woods

which father contributed. Mother was against it but father felt we must do everything possible to save human life.

The municipal building was surrounded by a crowd of Jews. Some came out of hiding; others returned from the forest to find their homes sealed up and their possessions taken by the municipality.

A delegation of men entered the building while the majority waited outside, discussing the deportation and the loss of their families and friends. I joined a group surrounding a municipal clerk known for his vitriolic tongue. He was in a bad mood and took it out on the assembled Jews. Accusing them of lack of subordination, he blamed them for causing trouble and told them bluntly that the deportation was still in progress. Therefore, he said, nothing would be returned by the municipality, and they had better disperse instead of bothering the authorities.

We listened, looking at each other in horror. No one said a word. Another shock followed the first trauma: this deportation was only the first in a series which would lead to the bitter, inescapable end.

It was obvious, under the circumstances, that my waiting was a waste of time. Drained of all my wits, I hurried home to share the news. A Gentile friend stopped me at the market place and advised me to leave Zwierzyniec immediately. Where could we go? I thought for the hundredth time. The only possibility was escaping to the forest. But even the local Jews, familiar with the conditions, seemed discouraged after only twenty-four hours in the woods.

Father accepted the news rather calmly. He didn't worry about immediate repercussions. Quite the contrary, he was confident we would now face a period of relaxation in which all restrictions would be eased in order to bring the Jews out of their hide-outs. Father was right.

That same afternoon the municipality was instructed by the German district chief to inform all Jews that they would be spared and used by the German authorities in local projects. At the same time, the municipality was also ordered to open the Jews' houses and return their possessions.

The German scheme worked once more. Almost all the remaining Jews came out of hiding. The municipality, unhappy with the change, tried to ignore the German order. But the houses were eventually opened and some of the basic possessions returned.

A few days passed, and Mira too came out of hiding. She returned home and told us about her ordeal.

On the day of the deportation, Zygmunt took her to his sister-in-law in Zawada. Olga's husband was away, and she was glad to have a companion, particularly when told she would be protecting an important participant in a sabotage planned against the Germans. Moved by patriotic feelings, Olga was outgoing and friendly. The relationship promised to be perfect until she heard rumors about the deportation of Jews from neighboring villages.

After a day, Olga's attitude suddenly changed from friendly to

The pursuit

suspicious. Because of her erratic behavior, her brother-in-law did not dare mislead her any longer and took Mira to a peasant, also in Zawada. The peasant, a father of small children, was afraid to keep Mira in his house and offered her a hiding place in his barn, which she gratefully accepted.

She stayed in a hole, concealed by haystacks, and was careful not to show any sign of her presence. The days were an ordeal and the freezing nights even worse. This, combined with the fear of being discovered and denounced, made her life miserable. She felt she would not be able to stay there long. When Zygmunt came to see her and told her about our return from the collection center, she made up her mind to rejoin us.

The danger of a second deportation prompted our decision to secure new working papers for the family. One of the most desirable employment places was the furniture factory, high on the list of German priorities because of its role in the construction of the nearby airport in Klemensow.

The factory was on the outskirts of Zwierzyniec and employed few Jews, mainly carpenters. Not discouraged by this limitation, we decided to try. At the gate of the factory we found a rather pleasant watchman who took my note to the director and promptly returned to escort us to his secretary. She made us wait in a spacious room, with modern furniture and posters depicting the Nazi conquest of Europe.

After a short while, a dark, middle-aged man with inquisitive eyes summoned us to his office. The director read my note aloud and asked for a few details concerning my training at the Academy of Fine Arts in Warsaw. After a long interview, he apologetically explained he did it only to satisfy his own curiosity and was not in need of a designer. All he could do was employ us in the factory.

We accepted his offer with gratitude and made sure we would be able to claim our parents as dependents. The director instructed his secretary to complete the applications and added jokingly: "Now we have our own furniture designer on the premises."

The job at the factory was wearisome. It was, in fact, so exhausting that we had a very hard time coping. This was partly due to our relationship with the Polish girls, who barely tolerated us and cleverly managed to use us for handling the most difficult assignments. They, in turn, hid among the stacks for prolonged chats with the male employees. The foreman, aware of this, found it convenient not to reprimand the girls, whose attitude was too well-known to him.

At the end of August more Jews were hired at the factory, and finally all the Jews who had escaped the deportation were encouraged to join its labor force. The change in the factory policy was so drastic that it gave rise to all sorts of speculation; but the daily worries left little time for reflection.

Father was once again summoned to supervise the Jewish workers. Now that the three of us worked in the factory, mother was alone with the baby in the house. During this period I rarely saw my son,

They loved each other dearly 87

who grew more and more attached to his grandmother. They spent entire days together and loved each other dearly. Mother read to him, and took him for long walks and to his favorite dentist, who had managed to return from the collection center.

Bobus was growing fast and was very bright. He loved his books and knew them by heart. Unable to find a book for his next birthday, I decided to write and illustrate one myself. My book was almost ready at the time of the deportation and was miraculously left untouched. Now it was complete and I was able to present it to my son on his fourth birthday.

The book dealt with one day in Bobus' life, the day he spent with Genia's three-year-old daughter, Bozenka. The cover portrayed two children holding hands under the title: *BOBUS AND BOZENKA*. The text and illustrations were devoted to their daily activities.

When Bobus saw his birthday present, he was so overwhelmed that he would not separate himself from the book for a moment. He carried it around, showed it to everybody, and continually turned pages, obviously enjoying looking at his companion and himself— walking, running, feeding the poultry and riding the tricycle together. At bedtime he hid the book under his pillow and in the morning asked me to read it to him again. He simply would not let it out of his sight, as if he were afraid of losing it, like his watercolor, which I once threw out. I will never forget the expression on his tiny face when I tried to explain that he had made the paper too wet and his "masterpiece" could not be kept. Very soon after this, my son proved to me he was, indeed, capable of creating a real masterpiece.

After the deportation, Bobus developed a greater interest in the boxcar trains, which resumed their route in front of our windows. One Tuesday morning, he joined me at the kitchen window to watch the death train, which suddenly appeared on the horizon. He grabbed a pencil and a piece of paper and drew his interpretation of the steaming and puffing monster rolling along the tracks. The drawing, produced in minutes—with spontaneity and an instinctive grasp of essentials—was excellent. It left us all speechless.

My son showed a great interest in my painting. He never missed an opportunity to watch me and imitate my work using my brushes and paper. However, his most successful drawings were created in complete privacy and appeared in the margins of his books and on torn-off pieces of paper. Among them were several superb likenesses of his teddy bear and his horse with head and tail—all complete.

These were unusual drawings for a three-year-old child, but the death train was something unique. It was a sudden outpouring of an emotion, which had ripened in him after the agonies of the deportation. Extremely sensitive and mature for his age, Bobus seemed aware of the peril hanging over us. He often argued with his playmates that he would never be forced to mount the monster train because I would find a way to protect him. But the fear, looming in his subconscious, suddenly appeared with unmistakable clarity in his drawing of the death train. The passing monster, with its long row of boxcars and puffing locomotive, couldn't have been rendered with more force and conviction.

Proud of his achievement, Bobus raised the drawing and exclaimed: "This is the train, you see—the train passing over there," and pointed to the box cars slowly moving along the tracks.

Bobus created this drawing on the morning of his birthday. On August 24, 1942, my son was four years old. Grateful to God for still being alive, we celebrated his birthday with a small afternoon party. The day was sad and full of recollections, but I decided to overcome my emotions and make it as pleasant as possible. I decorated the kitchen with colored paper borrowed from my neighbor who also supplied mats and dishes for the occasion. Genia brought cookies and candy for the children, and we prepared thin slices of home-baked bread with marmalade.

The children came in the early afternoon, and after consuming the sweets, sang the usual birthday songs, wishing Bobus many "happy returns." The celebration was short and the spirit dim; but Bobus was ecstatic, displaying his new book and pretending to read from it. His memory was prodigious, and as he turned the pages, he quoted from them. His performance was so convincing the children thought he was actually reading. When he put the book down, Romeczek, looking at him in awe, asked, "Can you read Bobus?"

"No, not yet," he answered, "but I will learn soon."

When the children left, Bobus urged me to read his book. Disappointed with my reading, he said sadly, "You must be tired Lolus, you just jumped a line." He was so right.

Several days later, Bobus contracted a serious case of diptheria. I summoned the only Polish physician in Zwierzyniec, who came in spite of German restrictions forbidding him any contact with Jews. His prognosis was grim, and the lack of medicine sealed my son's fate.

Our entire life now revolved around the factory. Almost all Jews

Bobus

90

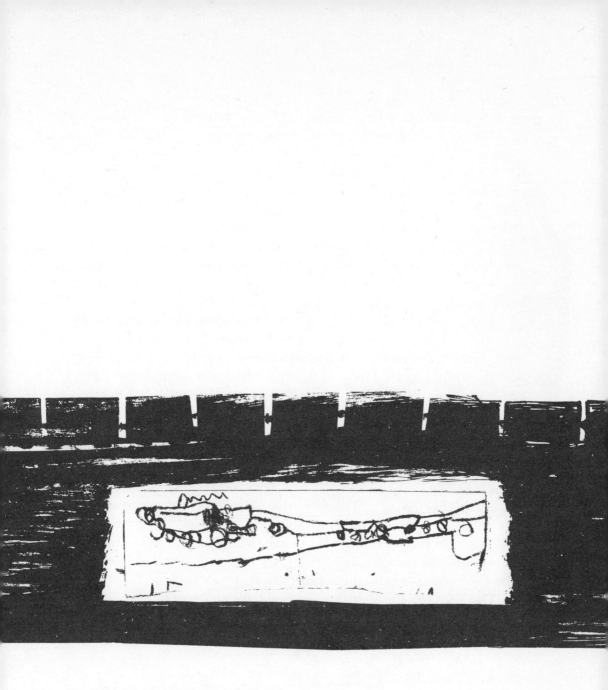

The "Death Train"
Drawing by Robert (Bobus) Michael Gurdus

capable of working were employed there and depended on the factory for food rations, supplied by the management. The Jewish rations, inferior in quality, were also only half the quantity of that received by the Poles. Each Jewish employee was given a few rotten vegetables, half a loaf of bread and five ounces of sugar for the entire week. Father, who supervised the distribution, devised a system of compiling rations for an entire family and thus simplified the tedious task.

But this was not possible in the case of old Shlomo, who, at odds with his wife, insisted on being served individually. After receiving his share, he would hide in a dark corner and devour the entire weekly portion of bread and later accuse his family of letting him starve.

Like most older Jews at the factory, Shlomo was unable to cope with the drudgery. Father asked the foreman to assign him easier work, but the director's instructions forbade treating Jews individually; they could be replaced only in case of sickness or death. The director was a Nazi who followed the party's hard line. He pretended to protect his Jews but actually exploited them mercilessly. Rumors circulated, however, that he had a Jewish university friend, whom he put in charge of an important project at Tarnowatka. He also brought a Jewish family to Żwierzyniec and apparently saved their lives during the deportation.

At the beginning of October, the German *Kreishauptmann* (district chief) summoned the representatives of Jewish communities to a conference in Bilgoraj. The conference dealt officially with ameliorating the working conditions of the Jews in the district but concluded with the compilation of their exact count.

Dr. Riedler, the delegate for the Jews of Zwierzyniec, returned from Bilgoraj with the firm conviction that this was the last German effort to nail all Jews to their places of work to facilitate the approaching second deportation.

Seeing through the German scheme did not make things easier, and reading about it did not change anything. I found a recent issue of *Voelkischer Beobachter*, addressed to the director, in which the writer quoted Hitler's promise to annihilate all Jews by the end of 1942.

It was October 19—Kuba's birthday. I took the newspaper to the director to get his reaction. He looked at it and answered concisely: *"Es wird nicht so heiss gegessen wie's gekocht wird"* (You don't eat as hot as you cook). The day was hot and the director was very irritable; he expected visitors and asked me to leave.

An hour later Prince Jan, with the Superintendent of Forestry, came to inspect the factory premises. The visit was obviously related to changes expected at the factory. The director led them through the halls, pointing out the people responsible for the various operations. When he introduced father, he was surprised to hear the prince mention their long-standing acquaintance.

In the afternoon things started to look grim. Bad news came from the village, signaling the approaching doom.

The following day father stayed home. He didn't feel well. His deep-set eyes were surrounded by black circles, and his haggard face had an earthy color. When he didn't show up at the factory, some of the Jewish workers thought it was because of the precarious situation. But he still didn't know anything.

We worked late and left the factory at dark. A motorcycle had stopped at the gate—it was Prince Jan. After making certain we were not watched, he told us confidentially that a new deportation was coming. Touched by his concern, we thanked him and were about to move on. But the prince unexpectedly offered us his assistance, suggesting that he could place us separately on two of his southern estates. Encouraged by his interest, I timidly asked if we would be allowed to take our parents along. He readily agreed and proposed to meet us on Friday at the same time, asking us to keep the matter secret. When Mira mentioned the problem of documents, the prince answered evasively, "Do I have to know the pedigree of all my employees?"

We hurried home to share the good news with our parents. They were waiting for us impatiently with Sam, a friend of the Riedlers who also had attended the conference in Bilgoraj, and was positive the Germans were planning a second deportation. When asked about his family, he told us that on his return to Jozefow, he had found his wife and six-year-old son among nearly a hundred Jews murdered by the Nazis in retaliation for one German killed by the partisans.

Sam's experience left me numb; his grief was so profound that it was useless to even try to console him. He spoke with bitterness about German cunning and cruelty and concluded there was no escape left other than the forest. Some of his friends had secured false documents from the Polish Underground; others had obtained authentic documents from Polish officials for exorbitant amounts of money. For him all this was a short-range rescue policy. He was determined to join the partisans operating in the district and left after midnight with his Jewish armband in his pocket.

Sam's tragedy and his evaluation of the situation made a deep impression on our parents. They were very depressed, and it was difficult to tell them about the encounter with the prince and his rather delayed readiness to help. Father refused to consider the offer; mother, discouraged by his reaction, ignored our pleading, although I felt her own attitude was more positive. We retired for the night with the bitter taste of vanishing hope.

On October 21, 1942, I awoke with a headache. It was useless to go to the factory. I went to see Genia to ask about news from the colonel. During the last few weeks I had tried in vain to get in touch with him. My telegrams remained unanswered; and when I finally reached him on the phone, he made a few empty promises. Genia, aware of her brother-in-law's responsibility and even more of his promise to help us, also knew that his wife and her sister had forbidden him to get involved with us at this stage.

Genia was not at home. I decided to see the Riedlers across the street. They were deeply moved by Sam's ordeal and found his decision wise. Mrs. Riedler, a gray-haired woman in her late thirties, was pregnant. Both she and her husband were employed by the colonel and placed their confidence in his ability to protect them.

While we spoke about the latest German atrocities in nearby villages, an office messenger, who just returned from Szczebrzeszyn, burst into the room and told us about the deportation: "The liquidation of Jews has already started in Szczebrzeszyn. The German military police, the SS and the Polish police surrounded the ghetto and set up machine guns at vital points. They proceeded from house to house tearing down gates and doors and tossing hand grenades into hide-outs and cellars. The Jews rounded up during the search were beaten, kicked and driven with rifle butts to the market place. Poles were threatened with death for hiding Jews, and those who assisted in the roundup were rewarded. Hundreds of Jews, dragged from their hide-outs were shot on the spot. They all looked terrible—the cruelty of the Germans surpassed all imagination."

I felt sick. I left the room and ran home. At the road-crossing I met Mira, returning from the factory.

"Do you know?" I asked.

"Yes, I do," she whispered.

We entered the kitchen and Mira fell on the bed. Mother gave her a cup of tea and covered her gently. Father did not want to talk. I

The round-up

Mothers

decided to go to the factory to see the director, who was an influential man and could help all of us if he wanted to. But would he?

The factory courtyard was filled with Jewish workers and their families. They all knew about Szczebrzeszyn and assembled in the factory to seek the director's help. Both the director and his superintendent had been gone since morning, but the foreman posted a note asking everybody to wait. The crowd was restless. The younger people felt trapped and considered escaping into the woods; the older ones still placed their confidence in the director and his promises. It was getting late and I felt a sudden urge to leave. Outside the gate I met the Superintendent of Farms, who knew about the situation and asked what we intended to do. "In case I can be of any help," he concluded, "come to see me at the farm."

Hurrying home, I tried to determine our chances for escape. They were slim. The prince promised to meet us on Friday. This was still Thursday and the Germans were expected here any moment. Perhaps we could hide at the farm overnight; but how would we get in touch with the prince?

I came home full of ideas. Father refused to listen. He begged me to stop and leave him alone. Mother felt the same way. After a long while father said: "I am mentally and physically prepared for the end. If you and Mira are ready for the struggle, then I am quite confident you will live to see the end of Hitler. I have the firm conviction that you will witness the end of his reign and the fall of Germany. The day of Hitler's doom is close and his star is already on the decline. You will live to see his end and this is enough for me. Mother has to make her own decision."

Mother remained silent for a long time. Then she approached father and reminded him of their vow to die together. They looked at each other with deep devotion.

The house was quiet; nothing betrayed the seriousness of the moment. Father was at the window; Mira was resting. Mother took the simmering pot off the stove when father called us to the window. Pointing at the row of Germans, hastily moving along the tracks in the direction of the forest, he exclaimed, "There they are, this is the beginning!"

Mother, outwardly calm, asked us to come to the table and eat the hot soup. A heavy sound of marching boots came from the outside and a group of Nazis quickly passed our windows, moving along the road leading to the forest. With fingers ready on the triggers of their guns, they charged forward like hunting dogs about to attack their prey; one of them wore a bloody red scarf around his neck.

Shocked by the sudden sight of the Germans, I knew I was not ready to submit to these murderers. "I cannot face them!" I exclaimed.

"If you feel so strongly about it, then take a chance, my child," said father.

"Go my dear," echoed mother.

I collected our papers, Mira's Aryan document and my Academy identification with slight name changes. Mother insisted we finish the soup, and father, watching us eat, reflected: "The first shot you will soon hear will probably be for me, unless they move me out forcibly."

"The second shot will hopefully be for me," asserted mother.

We sat, glued to our chairs, listening to them in disbelief.

"Give them your money and some food," reminded father.

Mother took out her bundle and divided it between us; I put a few pieces of sugar in my pocket.

"Keep together and watch each other," pleaded mother.

Father got up from the table and approached the window to check if all was clear. Then he embraced and kissed us, urging us to go. Mother accompanied us to the door and remained in the open doorway until we disappeared around the corner of the house. We left with the image of our dearest ones sealed in our hearts and minds.

The market place was full of Germans

CHAPTER FIVE

ESCAPE TO CHOBRZANY

WE HAD JUST TURNED into the side street leading to the market when a sudden detonation sent several shopkeepers into the street. The butcher, with whom we bartered our sugar beets in exchange for milk, motioned to us, shouting: "Don't go to the market—it's full of Germans."

The Germans were already all around, and a tall Gestapo officer, accompanied by a local Jew, headed in our direction. Pretending not to know us, young Biberman tried to divert the attention of the Gestapo officer, who slowed down and looked us over. Although he let us pass, several other Germans headed toward us.

It was dangerous to proceed, so we stopped at the house of a factory friend. Zosia, surprised to see us, opened the door hesitantly and made us stay in the kitchen, afraid to upset her ailing father. The old man, hearing strange voices, called her in, and she returned from his bedside, begging us to move to the barn at the end of the courtyard. Outside, we were chased by a barking St. Bernard, who attracted the attention of a German soldier posted across the street.

We had just reached the barn when a young boy appeared at the threshold, asking, "What do you want here?" Then he ran to the house yelling: "Mother, mother, two Jewesses are hiding in our barn!"

The barking of the dog drowned out his screams, but the soldier looked in again. The boy returned with his mother and Zosia. The stocky woman entered the barn lamenting, "Jesus, Maria, Jewesses in our barn; Zosia, please make them leave, or I will call the Germans!"

I pacified the woman, who agreed to take her son home and give us a chance to move out quietly. When we reached the gate, I realized I had left my identification card in the kitchen. Mira waited outside, and I returned to look for the document. After a lengthy search I found it on the floor. When I returned to the gate, Mira was gone. Trying to decide what to do next, I noticed Irene motioning to me from her kitchen window. She asked me to climb in quickly and told me that Mira had been interrogated by a passing German patrol, and after being cleared, probably had no choice but to move on.

Irene closed the window and lowered the shades. Her nephew Ludwik was stretched out on the kitchen floor, pretending to read. The poor boy was obviously afraid to move, realizing he too could be included in the deportation. Ludwik's uncle was employed by the colonel's office. He and his wife Irene passed as Aryans; they lived, however, in constant fear, particularly after the arrival of Ludwik, whose features revealed his Semitic origin.

A group of Germans passed the house. Irene sent Ludwik to the cellar. I followed him, and we sat on a pile of potatoes, looking out through the barred window. The maid returned from the market bearing a rumor that the Germans were threatening to inspect all Polish houses to make sure no Jews were hiding. Irene was frantic but when she spotted Mira returning she signaled her to enter the house. Surprised to find me at Irene's, Mira quickly told me about her encounter with the Germans and her luck with the Pole accompanying them, who decided that a tall, blond girl like her could only be Aryan. Trusting his judgment, the German let her go.

Shaken by the experience, Mira decided not to go on without me. We left Irene and went back to the forest from which Mira had just come. There were only a few Poles there, who remarked with irritation: "Look at this Jewess, walking back and forth." We ignored them and quickly left the forest, hoping to reach the fields. Crossing the main road, we saw a group of Jews who had been arrested. I remembered seeing them at the French prisoners camp but luckily none of them acknowledged us, and their young guard looked at us indifferently. Passing the ditch near the hospital, I spotted the dead body of Esther, covering her youngest grandson. When I raised my head, I   99 met the inquisitive eyes of a German hospital guard. Only a few feet separated us when a speeding car diverted his attention and gave us a chance to reach the fields.

The high wheat concealed us. There was no one around—only an old peasant harvesting his crop; he did not pay much attention to us. We passed the fields without incident, but it was still too early to go to the farm. Keeping at a considerable distance from the farm buildings, we decided to hide in the forest until dark. The coolness of the forest felt good after the hurried walk. I rested my eyes on the soothing greens, brightened by the patches of sunlight passing through the tangled branches. It was almost painful to think that the undisturbed beauty of nature was oblivious to the tragedy around it.

Gradually the forest became submerged in evening dusk, and dew appeared on the grass. It was cold and humid. We huddled close together trying to stay warm in the growing chill. Suddenly, the sound of crackling branches and quick steps drew our attention to a group of Jewish factory workers, who rushed through the forest and vanished among the dense trees. Jankel, the last in the group, turned when we called but did not stop. Soon the Jews were gone, leaving us with a feeling of emptiness and regret.

They rushed through the forest

It was dark enough for us to head for the farm. After the few quiet hours in the forest, the return to the hostile world was frightening. We moved carefully along the field path and entered the superintendent's house from the back. He appeared almost immediately and instructed his foreman to hide us. I inquired about Prince Jan, but he impatiently shrugged his shoulders, assuring me that the prince had quite a few problems of his own. The foreman hid us in a hayloft and removed the ladder to erase any trace of our presence.

The loft was cold and dark. Our physical discomfort intensified the feeling of despair. Unable to stop the shivering and the violent chattering of our teeth, we felt miserable.

Sudden lightning illuminated the dreary place. Heavy rain followed, and large drops came down through holes between the loose planks. We tried to find a dry spot but there was none. Water fell all over us, and tears fell as a release of our deep sorrow. This was the end of the day in which we had lost our dearest ones, and which forced us into an existence of persecuted animals fighting for survival.

The rain stopped; we covered ourselves with the driest hay we could find and slept. At dawn, we woke up—wet, cold and hungry. Mother's sugar was gone; Irene's cabbage had turned black. We tried to sleep again to still our hunger. The farm bell sounded; the courtyard was filled with animated voices and laughter. The farmhands left after a while but a few more hours passed before the foreman mounted the ladder to reach for a few bundles of hay. He returned with a pot of soup and a note from the superintendent asking us to abandon the hide-out by dark. The soup, mixed with tears, was bitter and salty. After dark we left the farm.

Adjoining the farm building was a settlement, built by the furniture factory for its personnel. We had a few friends among them: Jadzia, an orphan girl, who was living with her uncle and aunt; and Wladek, a young cabinetmaker, who often spoke of his readiness to help us.

Mira decided to try her luck and we started out toward the settlement, dragging our numb legs through the fresh mud. The dense fog blurred the contours of the cottages, making them all look alike. My sister's sense of direction was good, and she remembered the house she had once visited. Guided by instinct, she approached the cottage and gently knocked on the door. Jadzia opened it and cried out, "Mira, you are alive, come in, come in."

"I am with my sister," said Mira.

"Come in both of you," urged Jadzia.

She took us into the kitchen and closed the shutters. Then she introduced us to her aunt and went to get Wladek.

"You must be hungry?" asked the old lady.

"Yes, we are," admitted Mira.

Preparing the food, Jadzia's aunt told us that Wladek was sure we had been killed during the deportation; he had searched the entire village for our bodies. Minutes later he appeared looking as if he had seen a ghost. He stopped at the door, gazing at Mira and crying.

Wladek told us about the atrocities he had seen that fatal day and about the Jews, who were forcibly dragged from their hide-outs and chased to the cemetery, where they were killed and buried in mass graves. Even small children were killed on the spot, and many were thrown into graves alive. Wladek stayed late into the night.

Small children were killed on the spot

The next day Jadzia returned home from work excited. It was rumored that we were still in Zwierzyniec, and Zygmunt, the factory *Volksdeutsch*, had asked her outright if she knew anything about us. Jadzia was frantic and begged Wladek to take us to his house.

Wladek's mother received us coolly. She locked us in her guest room, which was separated from the family's apartment and admitted that she did it only for her son.

During the lunch recess, Wladek came to tell us that the Germans had raided the factory and found a few Jews hidden there. They also searched the village and found Yentl in the family bakery. They shot her on the spot and arrested Zosia, the new Polish owner of the bakery, threatening to execute her publicly to discourage anyone from harboring Jews. And during the night, one the the Wagner girls, who had risked leaving the family hide-out for water, was spotted by a ghetto guard, giving away the entire family.

Loud voices in the hall interrupted Wladek. He recognized the voice of Mrs. Adler, who had come from the forest to buy bread.

"Why should I sell you my bread, you miserable Jewess?" shouted one of Wladek's neighbors, to the loud approval of the others.

The same evening Wladek brought our clothing from Genia, with tickets and money for the trip. His brother Adam and friend Walas, accompanied us to the station. Adam lead the way, Walas remained in the rear and Wladek walked with us; they were all armed. We reached the station safely but decided to remain outside the waiting room. After an hour, the delayed train finally rolled in, illuminating the dark station. In a distant corner I saw the Riedlers, looking at us discreetly. They mounted the car marked "Lwow" and disappeared inside. The train was destined south, but we mounted it, nevertheless, to get out of Zwierzyniec. At the first stop we left the train and waited for the next one going north. Wladek stayed to see us safely on the train to Sandomierz.

Blessed darkness enveloped us. The lights were out and most passengers were asleep. All compartments were filled and several passengers slept on their bundles in the corridor. We found two seats and squeezed in between the window and a stout city official. We dozed off, awakening from time to time by sudden halts.

The trip lasted several hours and at dawn we arrived in Lublin. The platform was jammed with Germans, Poles and Ukrainians. They inspected our train, looking through doors and windows like sniffing dogs. A long freight train carrying Soviet prisoners of war was on the 103 opposite track. Many of the young men pressed their bloodshot, Mongolian eyes through the barred windows, trying to see the station.

Our compartment filled up again. The passengers talked about the political situation, the food shortage, the restrictions, and above all, the problems resulting from the massive Jewish deportations. They expected our participation in the heated discussion, but Mira kept silent and I read my newspaper. Our lack of concern aroused their suspicion, but the friendly conductor who came to check on us dispelled the doubts of our fellow travelers.

Late in the evening we reached Sandomierz. Here too, the station was closely guarded by police patrols, headed by Germans who stopped passengers to check their identity cards. The atmosphere at the station was agitated.

The presence of a young Chasid, who walked along the platform, was unusual. It was long past the Jewish curfew hour, but the Chasid, not disturbed by the presence of the Germans, brazenly displayed his strikingly white armband with the blue Star of David. Guided by premonition, we tried to avoid him, but the observant youth had his eye on us.

Following the crowd, we turned to the exit and got into the only available cab. Before we had a chance to pull out, the Chasid jumped on its steps. The driver greeted him with a hideous grin. During the long ride, the Chasid asked how long we were staying in Sandomierz. He offered his assistance in selecting a hotel, and when we showed interest, he instructed the driver to take us to a midtown inn; then he got out, thanking us for the ride.

The cab stopped in front of Hotel Polski, a dilapidated three-story lodging house, painted grey, with a dirty national flag suspended from a wooden pole. The hotel entrance was poorly lighted, and an elderly woman at the desk asked for our documents and payment. I insisted on seeing the room first, and the old lady got up reluctantly and reached for the key.

Mounting the crooked steps, she mentioned the scheming of the local *Judenrat*, who protected the rich Jews and exploited the poor ones. According to an informed source the Germans promised them safety for a daily quota of Jewish hostages.

The plan of the Chasid suddenly became clear to me. Without a word of explanation, I grabbed our documents from the woman's hand and ran down the steps into the dark street. We had just hidden ourselves across the street when two Polish policemen entered the hotel. We turned into a dark side alley and walked along the river to the main road where we stopped a peasant in a huge hay wagon. He took us to the crossing leading directly to Chobrzany.

The night was humid and starless. Heading toward the hamlet we entered a wide gorge. The road was deserted, and only after we had reached Chobrzany, did we learn that the passage we had used was known to be extremely hazardous.

Loud barking announced our arrival, and a patrol watching the hamlet stopped us to check on the purpose of our late visit. When we mentioned Marysia, a young man took us to the road leading to her cottage. We walked through the small village, with its wooden houses, square market place and picturesque church.

Marysia's cottage, which appeared quite shabby with its crooked doors and shutters, was at the edge of the forest. I knocked on the window and minutes later Wladek's sister opened the door.

Marysia looked very much like her brother, only thinner and smaller. At the mention of Wladek's name she asked us inside, lit a kerosene lamp, and looking at us carefully, asked: "What brought you here—are you Jewish?" Ignoring her question, Mira handed her Wladek's letter and said, "This will explain everything."

Marysia reached for her glasses and read the letter carefully. She folded it slowly and turned to us: "Please forgive my rudeness, but times are strange and one cannot be careful enough." Then she went outside to the shed and got a mattress, two pillows and a blanket. "This is all I can give you—I hope you will be able to sleep on the floor."

Marysia gave us a glass of milk, then went to bed, hiding Wladek's letter under her pillow. We knew Wladek had planned to write that we had been forced to leave Zwierzyniec, but we were unaware of the reason he gave his sister. Marysia had read us only one sentence: "After the search is over, I will fetch them." Anyway, she seemed happy at the prospect of seeing her brother, even at the cost of keeping us in her house.

The following morning the entire hamlet knew about our arrival. Marysia came under the direct fire of her close friends, who did not believe her story and advised her not to risk keeping undesirables— Jewish or not.

In order to throw off suspicions about our being Jewish, we accompanied Marysia to Sunday services. The compassionate, young priest sensed our problem and added a few words to his sermon on our behalf. He advised his congregation to respect their fellow men and not to condemn them too hastily for their beliefs and convictions. His effort proved beneficial, and the strained atmosphere around us eased. Marysia was happier and her friends stopped ignoring us. Nevertheless, we made up our minds to avoid them as much as possible.

We spent most of our time in the nearby forest and meadows. Passing townspeople often insinuated we were Jewish and little children sneered at us. Life under the constant threat of being denounced was rather trying, and we looked for ways of bracing ourselves against potential danger.

It was common knowledge that individuals suspected of being Jewish were put through a routine examination in Catholic catechism. Mira, who attended a Polish high school, was familiar with the basic Catholic songs and prayers. She became my teacher.

Life in Chorbrzany was quiet, and our daily chores, which we took on voluntarily, consisted of supplying the house with water and wood collected in the nearby forest. It was late fall; the trees had shed their leaves and the wood was dry. We gathered the branches for the winter, and Marysia was grateful for the help. She began to enjoy our company, and her son, Stasio, developed a real liking for Mira, who had a way with children.

One early morning, while taking the buckets to the well, I spotted a few faint silhouettes swiftly moving along the forest path. They quickly disappeared among the young trees of the dense birch forest. My heart stopped. Here too Jews were on the run. I hurried home to tell Mira about the familiar symptoms of an approaching deportation or one already in progress. The rumor about impending action against the Jews of Sandomierz had become a reality. The German phantom of death was following us from Lublin to Sandomierz, reaching for new victims.

Our situation became precarious. One hint to the police could get us in trouble, and in the general upheaval two more victims would be of no importance. Marysia came home at noon and told us that the Jews of nearby Klementynow were being moved along the road to a collection center. Stasio, released early from school, said the children had been dismissed and asked by the teacher to stay in their houses. Around one o'clock, Marysia's neighbors went to watch the deportation and insisted we join them. Marysia reluctantly agreed, and we went to the hill overlooking the road.

The sight was overwhelming. A gray mass of people—men, women, children—solidly flanked on both sides by the Polish police

and the SS, moved along the wide road. It was very much like the Zwierzyniec deportation, only on a much larger scale. Hundreds marched slowly in broken rows, supporting the old and the sick. Groups of Chasids kept together, wearing their black coats and wide-brimmed hats. Some carried holy Torahs; others, apparently caught during their prayers, still had phylacteries on their bare heads and arms. The pitiful sight of horse wagons loaded with old women and small children was painfully familiar.

Mira, shocked by the sight, lowered her head; I did also. We listened to the shuffling of tired feet, mixed with the whisper that accompanied the marchers like a solemn prayer.

An infant's shrill cry pierced the air. The mother, sensing danger, covered the child with her shawl, desperately trying to quiet him. Instantly, an impatient German grabbed the unruly bundle and dumped it in the nearest ditch. Then he forced the sobbing mother into a row of marchers, and when she protested, he struck her with his rifle butt and threw her unconscious body into another ditch.

Excited voices in the crowd were silenced by Germans shouting: *Vorwaerts, vorwaerts, los, los!* (Forward, forward, move, move!)

Minutes later, the laments of an elderly Jew, beaten by a husky SS man, brought the marchers to a second halt. The old man, apparently stricken by a heart attack, was unable to move; but the German continued to strike him. Trying to put an end to the senseless beating, the victim's son sent a powerful blow to the German's red face. Another SS man shot the young Jew in the back. He fell to the ground, covering the body of his dying father.

This time the stunned marchers refused to move. Women wept, children cried, and men seemed ready to revolt. The air was charged with emotion, but the Germans skillfully terrorized the marchers by sending a volley of shots above their heads; then they aimed their guns at the crowd. Once again their method of persuasion worked; the march resumed.

It started to drizzle. The marchers covered themselves and their children with shawls and blankets; the bizarre procession moved on and on, leaving corpses along the road. The sun disappeared behind the hills and the sky turned purple. Many peasants dispersed. Others followed the marchers, waiting for the loot, which accumulated with each bundle discarded and each Jew thrown into the ditch.

Marysia finally decided to leave after speculating on what life in the district would be like after the elimination of Jews. Tired and wet,

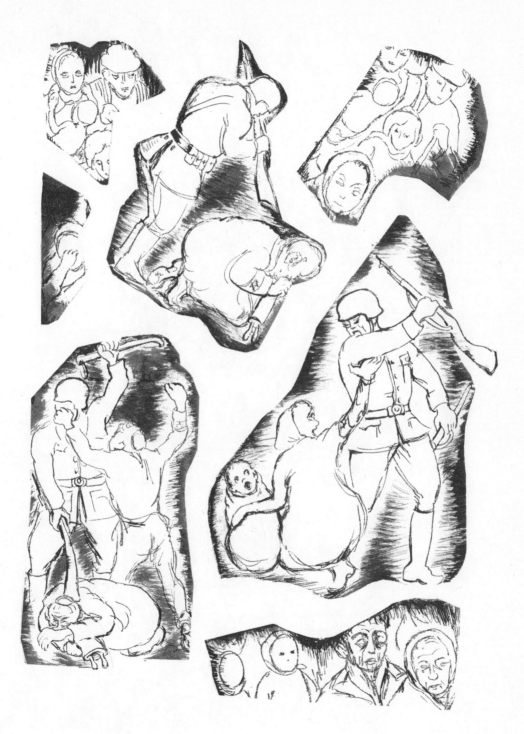

Forced halts

The march resumed . . .

we entered the cottage, trying to contain our grief. Fortunately, Marysia, depressed by the tragedy, did not wish to discuss the deportation.

We were about to go to bed when Adamówa, dressed in a tight jacket and a blood-stained scarf, walked in bubbling with excitement. Undisturbed by Marysia's astonishment, she explained that the scarf and jacket belonged to a woman who was shot. Her son removed it—together with jewelry, which would go toward the purchase of a new horse.

Not discouraged by our silence, Adamowa told us that her son had followed the Jews to the tracks and saw thousands of them collected from the entire district, waiting for trains supposedly taking them to labor camps. According to her son, the Jews paid exorbitant prices for bread and water supplied by the local peasants under the cover of darkness. "Some people have luck," concluded Adamowa. "We could also use money."

"Stop this nonsense," Marysia said finally. "I could never take advantage of poor, persecuted people." Adamowa, considering it an insult, got up and left in anger. Before retiring for the night, Marysia said her usual prayers and added one for the souls of the deceased Jews.

An unusual noise woke us up at dawn. I looked through the window and saw Adamowa's son harnessing his horse. He shouted to a neighbor, who was also preparing for the early escapade. With others, they went to Klementynow and returned in the afternoon, loaded with

Waiting for trains

112

furniture, bedding and various household utensils removed from the houses of deported Jews. Apparently the police had not interfered with the plundering.

That night the hamlet celebrated. The peasants, elated by their sudden wealth, tried to outsmart each other in the barter of looted goods. Some of them gambled with the stolen money and stayed up all night drinking and fighting. Those who did not participate in the brawl were scornful of their neighbors but did not interfere. Afterwards, guilty consciences and shame intensified the hamlet's hatred for the Jews, whose money was blamed for the corruption.

The atmosphere was tense. Marysia was nervous, and her neighbors were acutely aware of the presence of strangers. The hostility was growing and we decided to leave before something drastic happened. Marysia informed Wladek, asking him to come.

He came as soon as he could and brought two false *Kennkarten* (identifications) which he obtained for us from the underground. Marysia and Stasio were overjoyed by his arrival and proudly introduced him to their friends and neighbors. Wladek's presence added weight to Marysia's story about us, but there were people who suspected the truth. After the initial excitement wore off, Marysia, unable to hide her anxiety, asked Wladek to leave and take us along.

Wladek was disappointed. He had hoped that his sister would keep us a few more weeks and give him a chance to find another place. However, Marysia's fear was so intense that it left him no choice. We stayed a few more days, then left for Lublin.

113

CHAPTER SIX

BETWEEN LUBLIN AND WARSAW

W LADEK WAS AWARE that his association with us jeopardized his safety. But his concern for Mira made him indifferent to danger. He was anxious to find a refuge for her in Lublin, though his means were limited and he was lost in the big city. He also felt a strong sense of responsibility towards his family and was afraid of losing his job in the factory. Unable to do much, he decided to place us temporarily with a family on Pochyla Street.

Pochyla Street was notorious and inhabited mostly by railway employees. Wladek knew one of them, who, like his neighbors, rented rooms to strangers picked up at the railway station. Unable to question everybody, Mr. K risked bringing home many shady characters, and watched out mainly for Jews. Wladek was apprehensive; but the railway employee, not suspecting anything, gave us a room in his flat.

The following morning his wife thoroughly screened us. Wladek tried to convince her that we were members of the underground, which entrusted him with placing us in Lublin until the search for us had ended. Mrs. K was a shrewd woman but pretended to believe him. She warned us, however, that she would not tolerate boarders who interfered with her daily routine, and if we wanted to stay with her, we must get jobs. Wladek left, promising to see us soon and to help us to find the right kind of employment.

In the evening we met a few boarders who stayed with the family. Two women were Jewish, but it was not clear whether Mrs. K was aware of this. Pola, a brunette with classical features, had a sister and a daughter staying in other apartments in the same house. Pola's roommate, Maria, tall and blond, was fortunate to have a schoolfriend in the passport office who supplied her with an authentic document. The third woman sharing their room was Aryan but had a Jewish husband in prison. All three warned us that during the sporadic German inspections those without working papers were being detained for interrogation.

During the routine inspections by the Polish police, this danger could easily be averted by a fat bribe, which was always welcome. In order to avoid harassment, the family maintained good relations with the police and kept several members of the force on a regular payroll. This added considerably to their expenses.

During our stay, Mr. K brought home a family of two sisters and a child. Asked for documents, the women admitted they had none and were Jewish. Mrs. K scolded her husband and refused to keep them. The little girl, sensing trouble, began to cry, and Mrs. K, sorry for the outburst, generously agreed to keep the family overnight.

The following day, Alda, the family's only daughter, offered the two sisters unsolicited advice. She was a stout blond, selfish and fun-seeking. Her interest in the two women surprised her parents, who were used to their daughter's indifference to most matters. After a long conference, Alda offered to take the sisters to Lwow where they had a few Aryan friends.

Lost

That evening, Alda came home with three tickets for the night train to Lwow. The sisters were happy and grateful until she unexpectedly asked them to turn over their money and valuables for the duration of the trip. Astounded by the demand, they did not dare to oppose her and reluctantly emptied their bags.

At ten o'clock, Alda took the family to the station. She returned home after midnight with a wild story. At the station she had come under the scrutiny of the railway employees who knew her well and hardly missed noticing her unusual traveling companions. She found seats for the sisters, but before the train pulled out, the conductor asked them for tickets and identifications. Unable to explain the lack of documents, the women broke down in tears. The conductor called the controller, who took them off the train. "I really couldn't help them," concluded Alda tearfully, wiping her moist eyes with her fat fingers—studded with the sisters' rings.

We hadn't heard from Wladek and were discouraged by the inability to secure jobs. There was nothing left to do but get in touch with the colonel, who still lived in our parents' apartment in Warsaw. Mira volunteered to make the trip, insisting it was less of a risk for her because of her Aryan looks and because she had friends with whom she could stay. She was counting on one in particular.

During Mira's absence, Alda befriended me. She indulged in wild adventures and tried to use me for covering up her lies. Her parents knew little about her escapades and trusted her implicitly. I felt my friendship with Alda could easily get me into trouble with her parents and jeopardize my only refuge in Lublin.

Fortunately, Mira did not stay away long. She succeeded in getting in touch with her friend and received money from the colonel. She was in high spirits and insisted we leave the next day.

The railway station was exceptionally crowded. It took us a long time to reach the ticket office, and when we entered the waiting room, we heard that a detailed check of passengers was about to begin. Minutes later, the Germans started examining the documents of those passengers closest to the platform entrance.

The train was due in an hour, and we managed to stay away from the Germans who continued the inspection. Checking documents and searching luggage, they detained all suspects, letting the others pass to the platform. When they reached us, the train pulled in. The unruly crowd pushed forward and we eagerly joined them. At the platform a

German corporal approached us and asked politely, "*Sind Sie Deutsch*?" (Are you German?)

"What did you say?" I asked pretending not to understand.

The corporal repeated his question in Polish and demanded documents. I gave him my faked *Kennkarte*. He examined it carefully, and I noticed with fright that its crudeness did not escape his trained eye. He hesitated, then demanded working papers. I gave him my farm card, which had long since expired but which I had signed and renewed. The corporal sneered, and trying to take me by surprise, asked bluntly, "Who signed this card?"

It was clear we had the bad luck of falling into the hands of a shrewd professional with a keen eye. I hesitated, but Mira provided the answer: "The *Kreishauptmann*."

The corporal was not convinced. I felt the earth caving in under me when a group of young Poles, intrigued by the prolonged interrogation, approached us from behind. They smiled at us and we reciprocated. The German, slowly folding the documents, saw us smile at someone and spotted the group of Poles, who seemed to be waiting for us. Assuming that they were our traveling companions, he returned our papers.

The four young men, not realizing they had just saved our lives, helped us to mount the train and joined us in an empty compartment. During the ensuing conversation we learned they planned to visit the capital. When they heard we lived in Warsaw and might be able to show them the city, they developed an even greater interest in us. Grateful to our saviors, we gave them a fairly accurate description of the city's pre-war attractions, hoping some of them would still be open to visitors. The boys, excited at the thought of spending a few interesting days in the city, invited us to meet them. Without committing ourselves we promised to try.

The train arrived on time. The pre-dawn chill may have contributed to reduced security measures, and there was hardly a German in sight. We promised to contact our traveling companions during the day and hired a horse-drawn cab, which took us to the suburb of Saska Kepa. On Kryniczna Street we mounted three flights of stairs and rang the bell to an apartment, which became our main hide-out during the following years of the occupation.

A tall lean man in his mid-sixties opened the door. Stanislaw M greeted Mira cordially and introduced himself to me. His wife Zofia, a small brunette with hawk-like gray eyes, joined him in the foyer.

Janusz' parents were not surprised to see us; he too came out and greeted Mira with great joy.

Mira had met Janusz before the war. As I looked at this slender young man with olive complexion and expressive brown eyes, I could well understand why she cared for him. Above all, he had a free, friendly manner, which was quite appealing. He made us feel at home, while his mother returned to the kitchen to finish preparations for Sunday breakfast. At the table we were joined by the rest of the family—two boys, Tadek and Maciek, and "aunt" Dziuka, the family's housekeeper, who actually raised the four sons, the oldest of whom was in Russian captivity.

The meal was simple and the conversation casual. After an exchange of the latest news, Janusz took us to his room to decide what to do next. He had rented a room for Mira, and his mother agreed to keep me in the house temporarily. But this arrangement became precarious when the "ideological friend," assigned to Zofia by her underground organization, came to stay with the family.

"Mother," as Zofia was commonly called, was a member of *Armia Krajowa* (Home Army) and was truly inexhaustible in undertaking duties, one of which was the distribution of illegal, anti-German leaflets. Disregarding all risks, she plunged into underground activity to satisfy her thirst for excitement. She was a woman who never really grew up and had a constant craving for adventure. She had at one time been an excellent horsewoman, and it was common knowledge that she had admirers who avidly courted her—to her husband's exasperation. While Stanislaw was soft and gentle, Zofia was vain and ambitious and cherished her independence above all. She had a job, leaving the household, including the children, to Dziuka, who had a genuine affection for the boys, with the exception of Janusz.

Janusz had his mother's disposition, with all its spontaneity and susceptibility to nervous tantrums. He was difficult to handle, but Zofia adored him. Under the present circumstances, Janusz was certain his mother would help him accommodate us. This was, however, not the case. Zofia fanatically believed in her commitment to the underground and was afraid to disappoint her political friends even if it jeopardized the well-being of the family.

The first few weeks were relatively quiet. Then one afternoon, "Mother" brought home a short, middle-aged man, who was to stay with the family until further notice from the organization.

The family flat was small; all four boys had at one time stayed in one room. Since the oldest was gone, "Mother" offered the boarder his couch. The boys were unhappy with the stranger and disappeared for weeks from the dangerously overcrowded house. Dziuka was appalled, but "Mother" would not budge, hoping her noble deed would redeem the fate of her lost son.

The days dragged on in an atmosphere of uncertainty and tension. The new boarder spent most of his time outside the house. One day he returned early and complained of an oncoming cold. I offered him a glass of tea; he accepted gratefully and joined me in the kitchen. And in a sudden outburst of sincerity he told me he was Jewish and confided in me the sad story of his life.

In September 1942, the boarder and his family were picked up in the ghetto of Radom and included in a transport of people collected from Deblin, Lukow and Siedlce. After a long journey, their train was diverted to a sidetrack, leading to the extermination camp in Treblinka. Almost the entire transport, including his family, had been gassed in hermetically sealed chambers. He was spared from death by being assigned to the group of Jews who brought out the corpses to be burnt in huge ovens. After the long ordeal, he was finally transferred to the brigade which cleaned the arriving boxcars. This gave him an opportunity to escape.

Pale and exhausted, the boarder explained why he had confided in me. He felt that because I was Jewish, I would understand. He also asked me to keep his story from "Mother," and we parted with a strained feeling in spite our common bond and predicament.

After the boarder recovered from his cold, "Mother" surprised him with a request to vacate the room. Moody and unpredictable, she finally realized that the presence of strangers totally disrupted the life of the family. She didn't give the poor man any advance warning, and he left feeling bitter and predicting that I too would soon follow.

One morning the following week, while I was alone in the flat, the telephone rang persistently for over five minutes. My first reaction was not to answer; but the ringing didn't stop and I figured someone in the family must be trying to reach me, possibly to warn me against danger. Hesitantly, I picked up the receiver and recognized the boarder's voice. He asked about the family, particularly about "Mother." I hung up with a bad feeling and later shared my premonition with Dziuka.

In the afternoon, a penetrating ring of the doorbell announced unexpected visitors. Two civilians entered the flat and flashing their badges, identified themselves as secret police agents. For strangers, they were rather familiar with the layout of the apartment. One stayed in the hall, the other entered the dining room. They inquired about all members of the family, particularly about Janusz, and finally asked who, besides the family, was in the flat. Dziuka, bewildered by the multitude of questions thrown at her, didn't dare conceal my presence. The agents threatened to arrest me.

In the meantime, Mr. M had returned home and sensing danger, offered the men a bribe. They readily accepted, and it became obvious this was the sole purpose of their visit. I gave them the only piece of jewelry I still had; they grabbed it, promising to forget about me.

After they left, we realized they had been tipped off by someone who knew the house and had faked the whole "inspection." It was, nevertheless, dangerous to antagonize the impostors, who might retaliate by involving the real police. I instinctively felt that their visit was related to the morning phone call, but I had no way of proving it. Fortunately, the arrival of Mr. M and his diplomacy saved the situation. Neither the boys nor "Mother" had been in the house, and we decided not to tell them about the incident.

A week later the two men showed up again. When they entered the flat, I was in the pantry and stayed there during their visit. The door to the pantry was open, and one of the men looked in but didn't see me. This made Dziuka more confident, and instead of answering questions, she threatened to call the police. At the height of the argument, "Mother" walked in and grabbed the telephone to call the precinct. The men stopped her in time and left the house cursing.

After they closed the door, "Mother" broke down. She sobbed hysterically and insisted I leave the house immediately. Even her husband, who had just arrived from work, couldn't calm her. She feared the men might send the police and involve the family in real trouble.

"Mother's" anxiety was justified. Her husband also realized the danger but felt confident the men would not involve anyone as long as they hoped to gain something from the situation. But "Mother" anticipated the worst and could not control her nervousness. It was finally decided that I leave the house temporarily and stay with Mira until things quieted down. I left accompanied by Mr. M who wanted to make certain that I reached Mira's apartment safely.

My sister had rented a room from a widow who stayed with her family in the country. The room was on the main floor and faced the courtyard. Mira, under the constant surveillance of her neighbors, decided it would be better if my presence were concealed. This was not easy in a ground floor apartment, and I was forced to spend most of the time in a small alcove and use the bathroom only during my sister's presence. I got used to the limitations, but this arrangement didn't last long. The widow returned home unexpectedly and demanded that I move out.

After a relatively relaxing period, I was again homeless and without any immediate prospects for lodging. After exhausting most of the possibilities, I decided to try my luck with our old chauffeur, who now lived with his family in Warsaw and was the owner of a small factory. During the early months of the occupation, Jozef had visited father and offered his assistance in small matters such as selling some of our belongings to help raise money. I knew the man very well and was sure of his honesty and integrity. The question was, would he be able to keep me in his house for a while. Janusz went to see him in his workshop and easily got his approval to take me to his home.

The family occupied a small flat on Swietojerska Street. They had an extensive circle of friends, mainly neighbors, who visited them almost every evening to listen to their radio. Jozef was an excellent mechanic and was able to intercept the short and medium wave communiqués transmitted by the Allies to all eastern European countries. In addition to his popularity, which in itself was a serious drawback, the small flat was not conducive to secrecy. The two children, unaware of the reasons for my stay, tried to introduce me to the visitors which caused some trouble. Finally, Jozef's high-strung wife, unable to cope with her fears, asked me to leave after only a few days.

My situation was serious. I had exhausted all my possibilities in Warsaw and decided to try Lublin again. The lack of adequate working papers made the trip risky, but I had no choice.

They looked with interest at my bread

CHAPTER SEVEN

FROM PRISON TO CAMP

I LEFT AT DAWN to catch an early train to Lublin. As usual, the station was crowded and the train packed. In the overflowing compartment, travelers discussed the recent massive raids on Poles. Women, in particular, were now being picked up and deported for the depleted labor force in Germany. Hundreds were rounded up in the streets, movie theaters and restaurants. Janusz had mentioned these raids and encouraged me to take the trip, hoping that I might end up in Germany.

The trip went surprisingly well. But when the train pulled into the Lublin station, a platoon of Germans surrounded it and directed the passengers to the waiting room. After an inspection, only those with sound working papers were released; others were kept under guard. Again my papers were questioned and the officer in charge put me in the smallest group of suspects, destined for the Gestapo.

Escorted by secret police agents, we crossed Nowa Droga Street. The December snow was crisp and the sky bright. It was sheer madness to consider escape, but how could I not? Slowly, I worked my way to the last row and waited for an opportunity. It came when the stout agent, preoccupied with his pipe, stopped watching us for a while. A few precious minutes passed, and the group proceeded without me. I was at the steps of a long passage between buildings when the agent, sensing some irregularity, turned and spotted me. He instantly cocked the trigger of his gun and forced me to rejoin him.

The agent was furious. Cursing his miserable life and his lousy job, he blamed me for endangering his position and exposing him to reprimand or even imprisonment. He got so carried away that I almost regretted my attempt. While he was complaining, I decided to hide my cyanide in the half loaf of bread I carried for the trip, hoping this would not be taken from me during the search. The agent suspected I was hiding my valuables and suddenly assumed a protective air, warning me that all my possessions would be confiscated by the Gestapo and used as evidence against me. He then generously offered to hide my valuables and return them after my release. I ignored his offer, pushing the poison deeper into the bread.

After an hour we reached the brightly illuminated building. The agents took us to a room submerged in thick cigarette smoke. It had a partition separating the Gestapo employees from the secret police agents, who were sprawled along the walls on chairs and benches. Most of them were half-asleep, waiting for their assignments. A few turned their cruel eyes on us. Expressions of brutality and paranoia marked their haggard faces.

A Gestapo officer entered the room and the men jumped to attention. Assisted by an interpreter, the officer started the interrogation. When my turn came, the stout agent approached the officer and whispered into his ear. The German looked at me and had a short conference with his interpreter. Then the latter turned to me and asked a few basic questions, which I swiftly answered. The interpreter translated my answers into German but purposely reversed their meaning, while the officer watched my reaction to the deception. Outraged by the trick, I tried to be calm, but my face probably betrayed my sentiments. The officer, now sure of my knowledge of German, which I had previously denied, laughingly apologized for the injustice done to my answers and sent me to prison.

A tall German guard wearing a sheepskin and straw overshoes closed the heavy prison door and summoned the officer in charge. A red-haired sergeant, accompanied by a corporal, crossed the dark hall and approached us. He took the list of suspects from the police agent and studied it carefully. Then he instructed the corporal to inspect the men. They were ordered to empty their pockets, open their luggage and hand over their documents. After a thorough inspection, the men were escorted by a guard into the prison. The sergeant now turned his undivided attention to me and asked the stout agent a few questions. Listening to him, he checked the list again and concluded, "So this is   123 the case, she is suspected of being Jewish." The agent nodded and left.

Alone with me in the hall, except for the guard at the door, the sergeant raised his thick brows and smiling sardonically shouted: "Are you Jewish?" I looked straight into his eyes and remained silent. "Answer me," he yelled again, anxious to get my admission.

I did not answer and the angry sergeant, aroused by my disobedience, raised his voice, yelling hysterically. "Answer me, answer me," he repeated, stubbornly trying to break my resistance. Finally, getting no satisfaction, he slapped my face. The pain was penetrating, but the indignity much more humiliating. I raised my head and challenged him to a second blow, which he was about to repeat, when his attention was suddenly diverted by the opening of the front door. The tall guard admitted the prison commandant, accompanied by a high-ranking officer. The sergeant came to attention and followed the two men.

The prison hall was now empty and the guard moved from his post at the door, and after looking around, started towards me. At about half the distance he whispered: "He will soon ask you about your profession." At this very moment loud steps from the corridor made the guard jump back to his post. The sergeant entered the hall and asked me, "What is your profession?" From his post the tall guard was frantically imitating a seamstress. I got the hint, but the thought of serving the Germans, in any capacity whatsoever, was so repulsive that I preferred to describe myself as a saleslady. The sergeant shrugged his shoulders and took me inside the prison.

At the entrance to the female quarters, a buxom, blond matron greeted him with a broad smile and asked: "Whom do you have now?" The sergeant whispered into her ear, and she looked at me closely.

"All cells are occupied," said the matron, "unless you wish to keep her overnight with the women destined for the camp."

"That will be fine, but keep an eye on her and make sure she stays behind," ordered the sergeant before leaving.

The guard unlocked the door to a large cell, crammed with women. Most of them were sleeping on the floor. Some woke up, raising their heads to look at me. I approached the nearest group and two women moved to make space for me, asking why I was arrested. I told them I had been picked up at the station but avoided mentioning the main reason. They seemed genuinely sorry for me and reciprocated by telling me that they had been picked up in the street and kept the whole day without food or water. They looked with interest at my bread. I removed my capsule and shared it with them. One of the women was a young chemistry student, the other, slightly older, worked in a factory. After eating the bread, they started a conversation, and the student decided that the massive arrests were due to depleted labor in Germany, which had to be replenished by other nationalities.

I had heard that Jewish women with faked papers had been included in rapidly collected transports sent to Germany, where they were able to conceal their origin. I hoped this would work in my case. Unfortunately it was now certain that the women in prison were destined for a camp in Poland—not for work in Germany.

At dawn, two prison guards led us to the toilets, then lined us up in even rows and moved the column into the dark hall. The same tall guard was at the door. He recognized me; and when I passed him, he squeezed my arm and whispered, "That's good—that's very good!" It was surprising to find compassion behind a German uniform.

The guard was genuinely pleased to see me leave the prison, even though I was headed for the camp. He knew about the sergeant's orders and could have stopped me easily. Instead, he wished me luck.

An open truck was waiting outside. After mounting its steps, we were ordered to crouch behind its wooden barrier. Through the spaces in the partition, I saw a group of people assembled near the prison gate. In spite of the guard's warning, a few prisoners dared to rise and one was lucky to be spotted by a member of her family. The driver accelerated and took us straight to Maydanek.

Maydanek

Toward the Crematorium

CHAPTER EIGHT

MAYDANEK CONCENTRATION CAMP

MAYDANEK CONCENTRATION CAMP was on the outskirts of Lublin. The huge compound was surrounded by a double net of barbed wire suspended from tall poles and electrified by high voltage towers guarded by Germans with automatic weapons. Passing along the electrified fence I saw very few prisoners in the square fields lined with barracks. But their very size gave me an idea of how enormous a complex served as the extermination camp for the District of Lublin.

The Maydanek "death factory" was located on the largest field and consisted of several brick buildings—probably housing the disinfection and gas chambers. The one with tall chimneys discharging smoke was obviously the crematorium. A few prisoners, dressed in Maydanek's grey-black stripes, pushed a cart loaded with corpses toward it.

A shiver went through me when I realized with what cold precision the Nazis had set up their extermination machine. I could clearly visualize the masses of Jews who had once filled the now empty square fields. They had been murdered, and in several fields, heaps of their belongings were still being sorted by groups of Maydanek prisoners.

My thoughts were interrupted when we stopped in front of gate 13, flanked on both sides by guarded sentry boxes. The truck was admitted and pulled up in front of a brick house. An SS corporal came over to supervise the unloading and ordered his assistant to take us to the barracks.

We climbed the snow-covered hill, on which stood two rows of wooden houses. They were built of horizontal planks and occasional narrow windows. The houses were surrounded by deep ditches, accessible only by gangways, which made them look like small fortresses. When we stopped in front of the last house, the *Lageraelteste* (camp supervisor) ordered us inside. The barrack was dark. Small windows along one wall faintly illuminated the spacious interior, which was lined with five rows of triple-decker bunks. Scattered military blankets, gloves and socks indicated previous occupants and their hurried evacuation. The stench of carbolic acid was unbearable.

The women invaded the barrack and occupied the upper bunks. I settled for the first one availalbe on the lowest level and was soon joined by my two prison companions. The barrack was cold and its windows covered with frost. The *Lageraelteste*, young and well-groomed, entered accompanied by a *Capo* (former criminal) with a wicked face as red as his armband. She looked the prisoners over with her piercing, almost insulting, eyes and selected a barrack supervisor and two aides to direct the cleaning and the distribution of food.

The cleaning of the barrack continued late into the evening and was interrupted by the arrival of food rations—stale, half-frozen bread and cold tea. I swallowed my portion and retired for the night, sharing the bunk with my two friends.

The piercing chill, entering through the poorly insulated planks and windows, kept me wide-awake. Faint moonlight filtered through the narrow panes frosted with feathery patterns—giving the barrack a phantom-like appearance. Covered by the heavily disinfected blanket, I thought of those who had used it before. Who were they? Had they all been annihilated by the camp monsters? Were their bodies burning in the crematorium? Loud coughing interrupted my thoughts. My two companions had fallen into a heavy slumber. The faint warmth emanating from their bodies made me doze off for a few hours.

I woke up in the middle of the night, shaking and perspiring. The penetrating chill and the smelly blanket reminded me of my misery. I was probably the only Jewess in the barrack, packed with Polish inmates. So far they were preoccupied with their own fate and paid little attention to me. But what if they tried to satisfy their curiosity and denounced me to the Nazis?

Trying not to wake my companions, I slid down from the bunk and made my way to the entrance which was illuminated by a blue bulb. 127

Stumbling over bundles and shoes, I woke up a few women who swore angrily. Finally I reached the door and made it outside.

A dense fog hung over the fields and the pale moon peered out from behind a cloud. It was difficult to take in the staggering view—the vast stretch of land under the dark, starless sky, lined with rows of silvery wires illuminated by the dim light from lanterns suspended between high poles. Two revolving searchlights, manned by guards, roamed the field, forcing me into the shadow of the barrack. I scratched off the frozen surface and reached for a fistful of snow, enough to wipe my face and lick for a drop of moisture.

It was still dark when the bell rang and woke me up for the roll call. Two orderlies crossed the barrack, summoning the inmates with a loud *Aufstehen, aufstehen!* (Get up!).

Krystyna was asleep and her arm was nailing me to the bunk. Marysia was trying to pull on her stiff shoes. I reached for my clothing; it was frozen.

The orderlies urged us to hasten; but we moved slowly trying to gain time. By five in the morning we were outside the barrack. It was cold, but the biting night frost had given way to dampness. The morning dew hung on the electric wires, and a glossy surface covered the slippery snow. The inmates lined up in rows of ten and kept tightly together.

The field was huge, and each of the eight barracks was hemmed in by a wire fence. On the opposite side of our fence was the barrack of the political prisoners. They were already outside, shivering in their gray-black striped flannels. Some of them tried to warm up by hopping from foot to foot or beating their arms against their chests. I protected my frozen hands with a pair of gloves, made the previous evening from a pair of socks found in the barrack.

Hours passed and the *Lageraelteste* was still not in sight. The melting snow formed slushy patches under our feet, and water seeped through my thin soles. The women stopped stomping and stood around aimlessly trying to kill time and to guess what caused the Germans to fill the camp with new inmates. Having no answers, they blamed it on the Jews who were hiding instead of giving themselves up voluntarily. They considered themselves victims, caught in the massive action of bringing every last Jew to "justice." Listening to this, I began to realize the frightening power of the German propaganda machine, which poisoned the minds of its victims and turned people

128   against each other.

The women didn't know that after the Germans deported all the Jews, they began uprooting the Poles to allow German colonization of Poland's provinces. Entire villages in the District of Lublin had already been emptied of its inhabitants and replaced by German settlers. But the majority of the Polish population was unaware of the German master plan, particularly the women gathered in Maydanek. Few of them read the underground press which mentioned the present raids, prompted by an expected visit of Himmler to the major annihilation camps, including Maydanek.

The *Lageraelteste* finally appeared in the lower part of the field. She walked from one barrack to the other, taking ample time to check the prisoners. At our barrack she discussed the new arrivals with the *Blockaelteste* (block supervisor), and looking at the inmates, reprimanded them for their sloppy postures. "*Stramm stehen!*" (Stand at attention!), she yelled, not realizing the women didn't understand her.

The *Lageraelteste*, with her haughty manner and elegance, was shockingly out of place. This time she wore a grey uniform, trimmed with black and silver, and a white scarf draped around her neck. A forage cap, shiny boots, embroidered gloves, and a tiny revolver in a

Jewish prisoners from the adjoining compound

Jews in Maydanek:
1. Starvation

black holster completed her outfit. The *Capo* wore red trousers and a tight black jacket with a yellow armband and black swastika.

"*Stramm stehen*," repeated the *Lageraelteste*.

"Stand at attention," seconded the *Blockaelteste*, but the women were too tired to follow the order.

The *Lageraelteste* grabbed the *Capo*'s whip and used it on the first row of inmates, smiling when they screamed; then she left in disgust.

The roll call continued for a while until the bell rang dismissing all units. The women ran to their respective barracks to line up for morning rations. The door opened, and two Jews from the adjoining Jewish compound dragged in the heavy kettles. They lined them up for the orderlies and remained at the door, following the food with feverish eyes. They were hungry; rags accentuated their starved bodies.

130

Jews in Maydanek:
2. Degradation

The *Capo* entered the barrack. Seeing the Jewish prisoners, he screamed wildly, hitting them with a whip. Blood burst from their wounds, but not one sound was uttered. They huddled together and left in a hurry.

This time the ration included a piece of bread the size of a fist, a dab of tasteless marmalade on a piece of paper, and a thick beverage, which smelled like beets. Although bitter, the drink was hot and comforted my frozen insides. After we rested, the *Blockaelteste* divided the able-bodied prisoners into two groups. One was assigned to the barrack, the other to the outdoors. I was in the latter group.

Our first assignment was to clean the toilets. The job was unpleasant; the excrement was frozen and difficult to move—the smell was horrible. However, the exercise was beneficial. The toilets, located at 131 the end of the field, bordered on the electrified fences where a few Poles were making repairs. All of them wore white armbands, identifying them as outsiders. Aware of the massive arrests, they searched among us for relatives and friends. One woman attached a written message to a stone and managed to throw it into the snow without drawing the attention of the sentry. It landed near a workman who picked it up and nodded in consent. Soon after the men had finished, they were escorted by the sentry to another job.

The rest of the day passed quickly, and we returned to the barrack before dark. The evening meal consisted of turnip soup and frozen potatoes, a diet well-known and very much disliked in the camp. Again the Jeiwsh prisoners brought in the heavy kettles and stayed during the distribution.

At the sound of the bell, the inmates lined up for their rations. The first round was followed by an extra helping; a mob of aggressive women, pushing and yelling, returned for additional food. This time the *Capo* was not around, and the Jews waited patiently for the kettles to be emptied, hoping to find a piece of turnip or green potato at the bottom. The distributing Blockaelteste didn't give the two Jews even a spoonful of soup.

In spite of my hunger, I had to restrain myself from eating my potatoes, mainly because they were impossible to chew. I would have saved them for later, but a previous experience, which left me without food for twenty four hours, taught me not to leave anything edible, as there was always someone watching, eager to steal it.

I approached the stove hoping to brown my potatoes. It was surrounded by inmates, drying shoes or melting dirty snow for water. The stove was an ideal place for gossip, and while waiting for my potatoes, I listened to a lively exchange between the women.

"Imagine, they have already removed close to forty women from the barracks—all of them supposedly Jewish," said a perky little blonde.

"Many more," corrected her friend. "They took twenty from barrack eight alone and sent them to field three for gassing."

"Before sending them to field three," interceded another, "the Germans apparently used the young ones for games with their dogs."

I reached for my potatoes and left with the horrible news ringing in my ears. My heart was pounding so loudly, I was afraid it could be heard. Pretending to be tired, I reclined on my bunk and closed my eyes, thinking about the ghostly stories.

132

Jews in Maydanek:
3. Death

Jews in Maydanek: 3. Death

During the night, loud voices woke up the entire barrack. The lights went on, and a group of women escorted by two Germans entered. Still thinking about what I had heard at the stove, I was certain the Germans had come to collect all suspects. They had a short discussion with the *Blockaelteste* and gave her a list of names which she studied carefully. The whole procedure took a few minutes but seemed like an eternity to me. Overcome by anxiety, I began to search for my shoes. Then, I overheard that the women had been brought from the railway station, and the *Blockaelteste* was instructed to place them in the barrack.

133

CHAPTER NINE

RELEASE FROM MAYDANEK

T HE SEVERE WINTER OF 1943 made life in the camp even more difficult. The feeling of hunger was unbearable, and there was a critical scarcity of water. The deplorable conditions caused tuberculosis sending many women to the hospital. The situation became worse each day, and finally the Nazis decided to release all inmates legitimately claimed by their employers, local authorities or families.

The Maydanek Camp Command organized two commissions to interrogate prisoners, one from the District of Lublin, the other from the District of Warsaw. The commission in charge of checking the Lublin prisoners was headed by a major, assisted by his staff: a young captain, an *Arbeitsamt* employee and an interpreter. The *Blockaelteste*, an inmate, acted as liason between the Nazis and the prisoners.

One January morning the Lublin Commission made its entrance into the barrack. An armed guard remained at the door, and the members of the panel sat at an oblong table piled with papers. The *Blockaelteste* summoned all inmates to the front of the barrack but kept them at a considerable distance from the table. The younger women climbed to the upper tiers of the bunks to get a better view of the procedure. The crowd was unruly, but the *Lageraelteste*, assisted by the *Capo*, kept it under control.

Finally the Commission began the complicated task of screening the prisoners. Women claimed by their employers were the first questioned. The *Blockaelteste* summoned them, trying to control the uproar caused by each name called. Screams of friends accompanied and delayed the appearance of the inmates at the table. The impatient Germans watched the women with disdain but were unable to dampen their emotional outbursts.

The questioning of the inmates was a skill in itself. The idea was that the replies to the questions had to conform to the data received from the outside. After several hours of watching, I realized that the method immediately exposed each impostor, often getting her into serious trouble. The basic question asked by the Commission was invariably: Who do you suppose applied for your release? It was a simple

134

question for anyone legitimately employed before the arrest. For someone, however, whose family was trying to get her out of the camp by securing tentative employment, this question was difficult to answer. Some women were so nervous they had trouble understanding the interpreter, whose Polish was very poor; others were so confused they made an unfavorable impression on the Commission and were kept for further investigation.

The second priority went to women claimed by their local authorities; the third, to those sought by their families. Strangely enough, almost each case had complications, and after four hours of intensive interrogation, only fifteen women were finally released. I was pleased with the slow screening process and hoped the release of the 400 women in our barrack would take forever. I knew no one would try to claim me; but if this should ever happen, I would certainly fail the very first question.

Watching the panel, I made a thorough study of each member. There was the quick, alert captain, conducting the inquiry; the tense and sarcastic *Volksdeutsch*, translating; the moody and unpredictable representative of the *Arbeitsamt*, interfering in most cases, and finally, the frail, sickly major, who presided apathetically over the panel.

It was late afternoon when the first session ended. The moment the panel left the table, the roar of a hundred voices broke the tense silence. The women lost all restraint and followed the members of the Commission to the door, lamenting and begging for consideration. Some complained about their forced separation from their families; others expressed concern for the loss of their jobs. All pressed forward, disregarding the *Lageraelteste* and her whip. The guard opened the door, and the Commission left in order of rank.

The barrack was still bursting with excitement. The women talked about the interrogation and their dimmed hopes of regaining freedom. After the initial agitation died down, most inmates returned to their bunks to continue their discussions. I went back to mine and found my two friends excited and upset. We stayed up figuring out our chances for leaving the camp, which looked good for Marysia, a textile worker, but not too promising for Krystyna, a chemistry student. I did not disclose my anxieties and pretended to be pleased that the freeing of prisoners had finally become a reality.

At night I tried to think about my situation. Now that the Germans had started to free the prisoners, they would certainly release the majority of them; and those who remained in the barrack would be screened with particular care. I definitely had to leave the camp before this happened—but how? I felt I had to take a drastic step, which would be equally dangerous, but anything seemed better than passively waiting for the inevitable.

The second session came after two weeks; this time the officers were less inquisitive, and many more inmates were freed. They left after two hours with a score of free women. We followed them outside. The sun was bright and the snow was turning into slush. Not far from the barrack the major spoke to his aide, who saluted and left. He proceeded alone down the hill when a peasant woman approached him. The major stopped to listen but after a while, waved his arms in despair and moved on. On a sudden impulse, I ran down the hill, and to my horror, walked into a puddle, splashing the major's coat. He didn't turn and stopped only at the sound of my voice: *"Darf ich Sie bitte sprechen Herr Major?"* (May I talk to you, Major?)

The major turned around and asked: *"Sind Sie Volksdeutsch?"* (Are you an ethnic German?) Seeing my hesitation, he inquired politely: *"Was wollen Sie mir sagen?"* (What do you want to tell me?)

I mentioned my prospective position as Polish-German secretary at the wooden box factory in Lublin. The major listened attentively and seemed to be familiar with the factory, which belonged to the colonel and was part of the German military machine. Seeing his interest, I tried to convince him that my job was in jeopardy because of my unfortunate detention in the camp.

The major interrupted, asking for my name. Before I had a chance to answer, he apparently changed his mind and advised me to wait for the next session. Stunned by his sudden reversal, I stood watching him, unable to move. After a while I finally stumbled back uphill and realized with horror that a group of inmates witnessed the incident.

My prolonged conversation with the major showed my knowledge of German, which was invariably associated with Jews. All along I had tried to hide it. If the inmates now suspected me of being Jewish, they certainly had a hard time understanding why would I risk approaching a German major, and why he would be so patient with a Jewess. They must have been equally puzzled by my audacity and his reaction. The only explanation was that I was *Volkdeutsch*. But did the women consider it? At any rate, they looked at me with suspicion.

The discovery of my knowledge of German coincided with the unexpected freeing of our *Blockaelteste*. The women pressed me to
take the job, trying to tempt me with the special privileges that were

granted to this position, such as double food rations. It was difficult to resist the opportunity of slightly stilling my gnawing hunger, but the threat of steady contact with the Nazis was too dangerous. I refused.

When all settled down, I spent several sleepless hours on my bunk, thinking over the events of the day. To my chagrin, I realized my impulsive confrontation with the major was not only daring but dangerous. I was getting restless and was taking risks that could prove fatal.

It dawned on me that my carelessness had started some time ago when I put myself in jeopardy by asking an electrician working in our barrack to take a message to the colonel's office at Garbarska Street. He went there the following day and described my hopeless situation to a blond lady, probably Genia, who told him outright that she had never heard about me and accused him of inventing a story about a stranger in order to blackmail her. She even threatened to call the police. The electrician was flabbergasted by her hostility. I had a hard time explaining Genia's attitude and tried to reimburse him for his time and effort, but he flatly refused to accept any payment.

This experience clearly demonstrated I could not count on Genia's assistance. It was certain that if approached again, she would panic and deny any knowledge of me. This would arouse the major's suspicion and seal my fate. Fortunately the major had not taken my name and did not seem anxious to pursue the issue.

The Lublin Commission was due in a week. In the evening, I bought a pack of Yugoslav cigarettes from a political prisoner, wanting to forget about my troubles. The cigarettes were strong and affected me like hallucinatory drugs. They kept me in a state of indifference to everything around me, even to the white fat lice, which took advantage of my passivity and greedily sucked my blood. My head was spinning and I dreamed about my pre-war world—about home, Kuba and the baby.

Why were we so trusting and naïve? Why did we let the Nazis destroy us and turn us into human trash, into undesirables who had to conceal all traces of our real identity of which we were previously so proud?

Between cigarettes, I had lucid moments when I realized the game I had started was full of hazards; it could easily send me to the Jewish compound, and end in torture and death. I had heard many stories about the various torture methods the Germans used to break resistance.

Six long days passed since I had spoken to the major, and each day I felt more indifferent to my fate. Nothing bothered me any more—not the forced inactivity, not the hunger, not even the thirst caused by the nitrate potassium used instead of salt in the soup. I stopped melting the dirty snow and spent most of the time on my bunk trying to sleep.

On the seventh day the panel did not appear. In the evening the political prisoners from the neighboring barracks visited us, bringing illegal literature, which had been smuggled into the camp. The young, bright girl in charge of distributing the pamphlets was also known for her rare gift of fortune telling from cards. Seeing me smoke, she stopped and asked for a cigarette. I offered her a few and she reciprocated by predicting my future.

Stefania was an excellent fortune teller. Her reputation was well-founded, and she was also respected for her genuine interest in her co-inmates. She read cards for many of them and very rarely failed in her predictions. Fascinating stories circulated about her courage. She had been arrested for her underground activities, which she partly continued in the camp.

When Stefa singled me out and squatted on my bunk, many envious eyes turned on us. She didn't care and shuffled her deck of cards, spreading them on the blanket. After studying them for a while, she looked at me attentively and asked: "Tell me, have you recently lost a few members of your immediate family?"

I was stunned by the directness of her question and kept silent. Sensing she had touched a sore spot, Stefa did not pursue the matter further and collected her cards. She shuffled them again and asked me to cut the deck into small packs. When she spread the cards on the blanket, an array of red hearts hit my eyes. Stefa, impressed with the cards, said gaily: "These are the kind of cards I would like to open for myself. It's incredible how your fortune changes. It looks as though you will soon leave the camp, thanks to the help of an elderly man."

After Stefa left, the impact of her prediction took hold of me. I didn't dare move from the bunk and destroy the magic of her words, which seemed suspended in the air just above me. Afraid of breaking the spell, I surrounded myself with a thick cloud of smoke, which separated me from the others. Krystyna, who also had heard Stefa's prediction, was anxious to discuss the issue, but sensing my remoteness, arranged her place on the bunk and went to sleep.

Finally I dozed off, without covering myself. I woke up after an hour, shivering and coughing but inwardly quieter and happier than I had been for a very long time. Slowly I drew the carbol-fumigated blanket over myself and again tried to retrace every word of Stefa's prediction. The barrack was dark except for the blue bulb over the door and the prettily frosted windows. Watching nature's wonders, I dozed off again, blessing the long night.

I woke up indifferent to the barrack routine and even to a severe chest pain, which had worried me lately. The bell was ringing, and the orderlies urged everybody to leave the barrack, but I was still not ready. The last invalid was being helped outside when I finally reached the neatly formed rows of prisoners. My late arrival didn't pass unnoticed and provoked a biting remark from one of my neighbors: "Look at the Jewish princess—she finally made it." The women giggled. I pretended not to hear and looked at the *Capo* to make sure he had missed the insinuation. He did.

The girl's sarcasm had been carefully aimed at provoking an argument or fight. I felt it was best to ignore the remark; but this did not change the fact that my neighbor and her friends suspected me of being Jewish and might share their suspicion with the camp authorities.

I had noticed I was often watched by the inmates, who felt that I was "different," but nothing had been said in a direct way until this happened. Undoubtedly my knowledge of German created a great deal of speculation in the barrack. It seemed only the lack of absolute certainty prevented the inmates from making a final move.

The *Lageraelteste* arrived, and the women stopped their chatter. She called the roll, and for the first time the usual count was not reached. The roll was repeated with the assistance of the *Blockaelteste*, but the same four women were still missing. The *Lageraelteste* was furious and threatened to take drastic measures, blaming the *Blockaelteste* for the absent inmates. The *Capo* checked the barracks but couldn't find anyone. It seemed all possibilities were exhausted, but the *Lageraelteste* was not ready to give up and kept us outside. The sun came out and melted the snow under our feet, and the roll-call continued.

Suddenly, the *Capo* went to check the empty shacks further afield; within a few minutes, he returned with four women still half-asleep and wrapped in blankets. The *Lageraelteste* was fuming. Ignoring her rage, the women smiled at the *Capo*, who returned the grin. We were finally dismissed, and the women were sent away for punishment.

Before entering the barrack, I took a fistful of snow to melt. It was 139

Sunday and the stove was surrounded by a group of talkative women. The conversation revolved around the morning incident and a gentle little woman spoke wistfully: "This is not the first time these women have engaged in sexual activity with the *Capos*."

"This is because they are hungry," interceded another.

"We are all hungry," reacted the small woman, "but this does not turn us into whores and make us fraternize with the enemy!"

"Just wait until the political prisoners get hold of them," concluded a third woman. "They will regret they were ever born."

The heated discussion caused a mounting tension in the barrack. Most of the inmates condemned the four women; only a few tried to minimize the incident, blaming it on the circumstances. The argument came to an end when the rations arrived. Two heavy kettles were dragged in by the Jewish prisoners, accompanied by the *Capo*, who continuously prodded them, repeating, "You dirty dogs, you despicable creatures, move, move."

The scrawny prisoners, ready to collapse under the heavy load, finally put the kettles down, and the hungry women lined up for the bitter liquid made from vegetable extract, whose main virtue was its hotness. In addition, there was the gray bread and the marmalade—a Sunday special. I swallowed the beverage, already lukewarm, and took the bread to the bunk. Krystyna and Marysia were already there, busy cutting their rations into thin slices.

"Some morning!" said Krystyna.

"Yes, quite a morning," I nodded, thinking about my neighbor's remark.

"Imagine," complained Krystyna, "instead of attending Sunday services with my family, I am standing in slush all morning because some prostitutes missed the roll call."

"You have noble aspirations," injected Marysia. "You dream about church when I would gladly settle for just informing my family about my detention."

"Don't worry about that," said Krystyna. "The underground press has carried articles about the massive arrests, arranged for Himmler's visit to Maydanek."

"This may be so," interrupted Marysia, "but my family has no access to underground publications."

"They don't have to," explained Krystyna. "The news spread all over town by word of mouth."

"Maybe—but why am I still here, and why doesn't my factory claim me?"

"You are not the only one here. Wait patiently—your turn will come."

"But my factory is *kriegswichtig*" (war essential), pressed Marysia.

The talking went on and on and made me think about my family, about my baby, and about my parents, who had probably been killed in cold blood by the Nazis or forced to travel to a concentration camp like this—but to the Jewish compound with gas chambers and crematoria.

The Sunday quiet was interrupted by the arrival of the Lublin Commission. It was headed by the major, whose pale face betrayed indisposition. The *Lageraelteste* remained at the door, and the *Block-aelteste* moved the inmates to the front of the barrack. First summoned to the table was a tall, dark woman from the vicinity of Lublin, who had previously been turned down by the Commission because her answers conflicted with the information in the petition claiming her. The woman apparently had no immediate family and didn't know who had tried to get her out. Nervous and confused, she disappointed the panel and was kept for further interrogation. Watching her, I could see myself in a similar situation.

The next was a stout peasant, who approached the table with a loaded food basket. The major, intrigued by her robust appearance, started to question her through an interpreter.

"Where were you arrested?" he asked.

"On the train to Lublin," answered the woman.

"Why did you travel?"

"To sell my farm products in the city."

The major, apparently amused by her naïvete, put on a stern face and asked loudly: "Don't you know that under the present law food peddling is punishable by incarceration?" The woman gasped and started to lament, invoking all saints to her rescue. The major, annoyed by her outburst, sent her back to her bunk. But the woman pretending not to understand, became hysterical, and her cries started a chain reaction among the other women. A hundred voices, choking with emotion, filled the barrack. The *Lageraelteste* tried to stop the outburst, but her voice was drowned out in the uproar. Suddenly the major, stiff and tense, got up and thundered: "*Ruhe, Ruhe*" (Silence, silence).

All stopped. The major, breathing heavily, pushed his chair aside and approached the nearest bunk, motioning to the young women in

141

the upper berth. They climbed down and followed him to the table. An assistant examined their papers and handed them to the major, who freed all four. He then asked for the list of the disabled and without formalities, included them in the group of released prisoners.

The session was terminated; the panel got up. I used the opportunity to remind the major about my existence and uttered in one breath: *"Herr Major, Ich sollte mich bei Ihnen melden"* (Major, I was supposed to report to you). Still annoyed by the tumultuous session, he answered harshly: *"Die Fabrik wird wohl ohne Sie arbeiten"* (The factory will do without you). His arrogance destroyed all my illusions. Numb with resignation, I watched him disappear through the door.

All the devil's forces broke loose in the barrack. The women blamed each other for their predicament. The tall brunette was the first attacked by a group of young girls. A redhead accused her of being Jewish and was anxious to prove her point. The insulted woman was not ready to answer the challenge and put the blame for the turmoil on the stout peasant. But the redhead was not easily appeased and thundered: "It's you and others like you who make us stay here indefinitely. Why don't you admit that you are Jewish and stop wasting everybody's time!"

"It's you who are Jewish, and I sincerely hope you will never leave the camp," snapped back the dark girl.

The fight attracted many women, hoping for a spectacle. Bitter and restless, they eagerly looked for distraction and fought each other at the slightest provocation. The gravest offense was to be accused of being Jewish. To ignore the accusation was, according to the camp code, an admission of guilt. Aware of this I tried to stay out of sight until the attack subsided.

The atmosphere in the barrack was explosive. Hot tempers caused outbursts of violence, and only the intervention of the political prisoners prevented serious trouble. Because of their authority, many threats died within the barrack walls. The political prisoners partly succeeded in persuading the others that their duty was to preserve solidarity and oppose the enemy by passive resistance; they emphasized the point that to collaborate with the Nazis, even in exposing Jews, was unpatriotic and wrong.

But the inmates' hatred was growing. They were ready to punish all those, who, according to their judgment, had contributed to their 142 prolonged stay in the camp and were convinced that their misery would automatically end as soon as all Jews were exposed. Their minds poisoned by the Germans, they lost all reason and restraint.

It was late afternoon when the militant women dispersed and retired to their bunks to vent personal grievances. My bunk companions had gone to another barrack to visit a sick friend and were due back for evening rations. Seeing me alone, Zosia, a bunk neighbor, decided to share the latest gossip with me. Young but ugly, with pimpled skin and bleached hair, she snooped around the barrack and was at all times readily at the service of the *Blockaelteste*, who rewarded her with the surplus bread and soup she distributed among friends and helpers.

Zosia had tried to approach me many times and often watched me with her sly eyes. So far, I had diplomatically discouraged her advances; but this time she simply squatted on my bunk and lowered her voice to tell me about her most recent instructions from the *Blockaelteste*—to be on the lookout for Jewesses hiding among the inmates. She heard the insinuations and considered it her duty to warn me. It was clear Zosia suspected me of being one of the undesirables and was anxious to see my reaction. Used to friendly warnings, I remained composed, surprising her with my indifference. Disappointed at not being able to arouse my interest, she still waited for my thanks; but I skilfully diverted the chat to the dreadful conditions in the camp.

Krystyna and Marysia returned earlier than expected rescuing me from the intruder. They were animated by the good news from a recent secret bulletin stating that all hastily-arrested Maydanek prisoners had proven a burden to camp officials and would soon be released.

In spite of the good news, not much changed in the camp routine. New prisoners, mainly smugglers and prostitutes, were brought nightly to the barracks; the place was overflowing with inmates, making food even more scarce. The drastic food shortage and the unsanitary conditions caused an epidemic of stomach illness, characterized by vomiting and nausea, which sent several inmates to the hospital.

The only encouragement came from a warming trend in the weather which eased the grip of winter. The thick ice melted around the single water pump in our field, and ice-cold water was now available. This was a rare treat after the salted "coffee" and melted snow. It was impossible to resist, even if it required waiting in line.

On the first day, the queue at the pump was tremendous. I took the largest dish available and volunteered to get water for the three of us. Inmates from various barracks were lined up for half a mile, patiently waiting for water. Behind me stood two attractive women who looked like mother and daughter. They whispered not realizing I was able to hear most of the conversation. The older woman discussed the intensified search for Jews in the barracks; and the younger woman mentioned the latest toll in which twenty women had been taken to "Compound Three," including five from her barrack. They implored each other to remain calm and confident. My heart was aching for the two women, and I was anxious to warn them to be more careful in the future. On the other hand, I didn't want to alarm them and was afraid of being too concerned with strangers, bearing in mind Zenia's warning to mind my own business if I ever hoped to survive the war. I filled my dish and hurried to the barrack. All evening I thought about the two women. I was in the same boat but considered myself fortunate not to have anyone in the camp to worry about.

After I fell asleep, an exceptionally loud bang on the door woke the entire barrack. The lights went on and the *Blockaelteste*, summoned by two husky SS men, read a list of prisoners assigned for relocation. The last name on the list seemed familiar; half-asleep, I heard "Gierdaszowska," the name appearing on my forged *Kennkarte*. Not being absolutely certain, I didn't move. A shuffling about in the barrack suggested that the prisoners called were obeying the order. All of them reported at the door, and among them was the tall, dark woman from the Lublin area.

The Germans checked their names and demanded that the missing prisoner report immediately. The *Blockaelteste* repeated my name, and this time it came through clearly. My heart was pounding and I felt sick. Covered with perspiration, I listened to the German's shouting, but the *Blockaelteste* was helpless and assured him she didn't know anyone by that name in the barrack. The Germans insisted the prisoner had to be found and instructed her to check all women.

The day I had been dreading arrived. I was on the list of Jewish suspects. When I had ventured to "escape" from prison, I sensed that one day the sergeant would look for me. This made me cautious from the start, and the name I used in the camp had no relation whatsoever to the one appearing on my document. I hoped that at an inquiry this would protect me from inmates who could incriminate me. My idea paid off, and the bewildered *Blockaelteste* was at a loss when asked for a name she had never seen or heard. So far I was safe, but the incident made me aware that my document had no value and carried an automatic indictment. It had to be destroyed before being discovered on me.

Several days passed and nothing happened. I still had my *Kennkarte* hidden under the mattress. I was reluctant to destroy my only document and secretly hoped the Germans would not return and that the incident would be forgotten.

One day a few *Arbeitsamt* officials came from Warsaw to claim all those who had been arrested in the Warsaw District. The largest barrack was selected, and only the prisoners involved were allowed to participate in what was expected to be the first mass release in Maydanek.

I ventured entering the barrack and found a large crowd waiting for the Nazis. In contrast to the Lublin Commission, this one, consisting of four high ranking SS men and three *Arbeitsamt* officials, devised an efficient clearing system and freed over sixty women in two hours. The Commission recessed; the barrack was in a state of great excitement. The freed prisoners were immediately surrounded by the others, who wanted to send messages to Warsaw.

Looking for someone who would inform Mira about my detention, I moved forward when suddenly two fat lice crawled out from under an inmate's collar. The sight of these parasites made me so nauseous I almost vomited. I approached the sentry, begging him to let me out. He hesitated for a moment but realized it was an emergency and opened the door. Once outside, I quickly recovered but lost the desire to return to the crowded room. I longed for a rest and went back to our barrack. When I entered, I was confronted by an unusual silence. The Lublin Commission, which was in session, was just getting up to leave after freeing a number of women. The major passed me at the door and asked with astonishment: "Are you still here?" I followed him outside.

"By the way," he added, "did you notice the factory at Garbarska was severely damaged in a recent fire?"

I looked at the skyline with the clearly distinguishable contours of the factory and replied: "The buildings seem to be intact."

"Yes, but only on the outside; the inside is all burned out," snapped the major and left to catch up with the other members of the Commission, who were heading for the next barrack.

Pondering the meaning of the strange conversation, I felt a pair of inquisitive eyes resting upon me. One of the political prisoners approached me and asked, "The major seems to care about you; why don't ask him to free you?"

"I suppose if he really wanted to release me, he would do it without my asking."

The young woman nodded and said, "I suppose you're right. However, don't waste this opportunity. Go and ask him—I would."

Not certain this was the right thing to do, I was encouraged by the girl's interest and realized my laxity was not prudent under the circumstances. I had lost an opportunity and another might not come soon.

The afternoon sun cast long blue shadows on the deserted field, which was divided into two parts by the barbed wire fence. The new snow, covering the hill, was unmarred except for the footprints left by the Commission and the women who had trampled along the narrow path leading to the camp office.

I was inspired by my friend but not ready to follow her advice. It was clear the major associated me with the factory at Garbarska but still hesitated to free me; he seemed to have a reason. My new friend didn't understand why I was being cautious. She began crossing the field and encouraged me to follow. We stopped at a considerable distance from the barrack and waited.

A long time passed and the sun hid behind a cloud. It was cold and my friend was getting restless. Suddenly the door opened, and a dozen women raced down the steps. The members of the Commission followed; the last was the major. He turned to the released women and asked: "Does anyone speak German?"

There was no reply, and the major looked up and spotted me at the fence. He raised his voice and shouted, "You there, you speak German, come here!" When I approached him he ordered, "Count the women." After I counted, I muttered, "There are thirteen . . ."

"And you are the fourteenth. Take them to the office."

"You mean, I am free?"

"Yes, you are free," confirmed the major.

Carried by secret wings, I easily jumped the fence and rushed into the barrack to grab my bundle, hidden under the mattress. Krystyna and Marysia were already gone. Without uttering a sound to others I ran out, afraid of being stopped by the feared, "You Jew."

The major had left and the thirteen women were waiting. After a quick good-bye to my friend, I gave her my gloves and promised to contact her parents.

Leading the women along the narrow path, I passed, for the last time, the long line of huts, the high voltage fences, and the watch towers, connected by rows of barbed wire.

The brick building housing the Gestapo office was well lighted.

146   The *Lageraelteste*, busy at her desk, hardly raised her head. She or-

dered us to sit on long benches, which were partly occupied by the Warsaw inmates who were waiting to be escorted to the railway station and put on a train home. After an hour, the Lublin Commission appeared with another dozen free women. The *Lageraelteste* instructed the *Capo* to check our belongings while she gave us a thorough body search. No one bothered to recheck our identities, which as a rule was done by the Commission. After the check we were taken outside by a sentry. He informed the two guards at the gate, who in turn signaled the watch towers. The gate opened and a feeling of ecstasy went through my entire being. Free, free again. I could hardly believe it was real.

We plodded through sleet and mud on the Maydanek road. The sleigh carrying members of the Lublin Commission passed us, and the driver stopped to advise us to take the field road leading directly to Lublin.

Slowly walking along the snow covered road, I turned for a last look at the camp. It was submerged in darkness; the crematoria discharged a mass of thick, black smoke.

Struggling through the snow, deep at times, we reached the village of Dziesiatka, which was almost half-way between the camp and the town. The village was deserted except for a few peasants, who remained on guard and advised us to continue along the road leading to the outskirts of the city.

We reached Lublin shortly before curfew and attracted the attention of the few passers-by, who stopped to ask about the camp. I slipped away and entered the nearest apothecary to telephone Genia and alert her about a possible inquiry from the major. Genia seemed genuinely moved by my plight and promised to provide me with working papers, which would protect me in the future. It became late, and I was forced to try Pochyla Street for overnight lodging.

The K family greeted me with joy and were surprised to hear about my ordeal in the camp. They responded by complaining about their increasing problem with the secret police. I regretted having come, but I was too exhausted to run to the station and hoped to get employment papers the following day. In the meantime, I had nothing to show, not even a scrap of paper proving I had just been released from the camp.

Alda walked in looking prosperous. She was anxious to hear about my trial in the camp and made me listen to her newest adventure. I wanted to go to bed, but the family insisted I join them for supper. 147

Mrs. K put a plate of potato soup in front of me and encouraged me to eat. I was afraid to, but the smell of the soup was tempting and I took a few spoonfuls. The reaction was violent. Nauseous and damp with perspiration, I had to stop eating and apologized for the disturbance. Alda offered me her bed for the night and went to sleep on the couch. It was a wonderful sensation to stretch out on the fresh linen and rest my head on a real pillow. As soon as I lay down, I was sound asleep.

Early in the morning I decided to forget about the employment papers and go back to Warsaw. At the railway station I met the Maydanek inmates still waiting to be put on a train to Warsaw. Around ten o'clock a special attendant collected all released prisoners and instructed the train conductor to assign them to several compartments. We traveled in a festive mood, treated to food and drink by passengers. Still intoxicated by my miraculous return to freedom, I was eager to participate in the gaiety. It was so good to be free, even if it was only temporary.

The feeling of security dulled my senses, and I wished I could stay in this state forever. Time flew quickly—this time too fast for me. Afraid of the harsh reality that waited for me at the end of the journey, I had mixed feelings when the train pulled into the station. Some of my traveling companions were met by their families; the reunions were moving.

I hired a horse-drawn carriage with a girl I had met on the train, and we moved into the dark streets. A few policemen stopped the carriage but let us proceed after the driver confirmed we belonged to a group of prisoners released from Maydanek.

In Saska Kepa we stopped at the girl's address and then on to Poselska Street. When the driver disappeared, I went to Mira's ground floor apartment and gently knocked at the window. She responded instantly.

"I knew it was you," she muttered, trying to suppress her emotion.

"I'm glad you heard me," I said. "I hope I didn't wake your landlady."

"You couldn't—she is not in town."

The next few days were peaceful and gave me a chance to recover. Mira tried to feed me well, and I gradually regained some of my strength. We spoke about our prospects for the immediate future and Mira's recent experiences.

After the "Second Liquidation" in the Warsaw Ghetto, the Germans, aware that some of the Jews had succeeded in escaping to the Aryan side, had intensified their search and alerted the Polish police to watch for strangers in their precincts. Policemen, well acquainted with the permanent residents of Saska Kepa, stopped Mira for interrogation. They checked her registration and her *Kennkarte* and questioned her lack of employment papers. Mira's impeccable Aryan appearance saved her, but some of her friends disappeared without a trace. One of them was Krysia, who had just left the ghetto. Previous to her arrest, she had spent a few days with Mira and told her about the conditions there.

According to Krysia's information, Himmler's visit on January 9, 1943, sealed the fate of the Warsaw Ghetto. The January Revolt, prompted by the "Second Liquidation," made the Germans aware of the new Jewish resistance forces. Determined to empty the ghetto, the Germans embarked on a peaceful evacuation plan, hoping to force the remaining 40,000 Jews from their strongholds. Most of these Jews were employed in German factories.

One of the major employers was Walter Caesar Toebbens, who was ordered by the Germans to move his factory to the countryside, with the Jewish workers and their families. Toebbens was used by the Nazis to advertise the advantages of new working conditions outside Warsaw. However, the Jewish Fighting Organization called on all ghetto Jews to ignore the propaganda, stressing that "peaceful resettlement" was nothing but a new form of extermination.

Before her disappearance, Krysia, herself a member of the Fighting Organization, told Mira that the fight between the German propaganda machine and her organization was in progress; regardless of the outcome, Jewish youth in the ghetto were determined to put up a last fight for survival.

Ghetto fighters

CHAPTER TEN

FROM PLACE TO PLACE

At THE BEGINNING OF APRIL, Mira's landlady returned from the farm and found me in the apartment. Mira explained I was spending a few days with her. Distrustful because of the previous encounter, the woman again demanded that I leave. I called my friend Eva with whom I had been quite close at the Academy of Fine Arts. She came promptly, only to tell me that she would gladly help but had no right to expose her parents to danger. A few days passed, and the impatient landlady threatened to inform the police and cancel Mira's lease. I had no choice but to try Kryniczna Street again.

In the evening, pretending to leave for the station, I took my suitcase and accompanied by Mira walked the few blocks separating the two apartments. Dziuka answered our knock and took us to the dining room where the entire family was assembled at the table.

150

"Mother" entered from the kitchen and invited us for supper. The family hadn't seen me for a long time and were anxious to hear about my experience in the camp. "Mother," deeply religious, considered my release a true miracle.

Time moved along in friendly conversation, and soon it was almost the curfew hour. Mira, ready to leave, went to the kitchen to talk about my situation to "Mother," who said I could stay temporarily but should definitely look for something else. Overcome by gratitude, I joined her in the kitchen to clean up after supper. It was like old times again.

After the family retired, I entered the room previously shared with Dziuka. The shades were not drawn and the room was illuminated by an artificial glow. I approached the balcony door and saw the sky reflecting a red glare. The Warsaw Ghetto was ablaze. I opened the door, and the wind blew smoke and soot from the burning houses in my direction. A few German planes circled the sky, dropping incendiary bombs on the ghetto.

Ghetto ablaze

151

I couldn't tear myself away from the frightening view and did not notice Dziuka had joined me. "It's late," she said. "You should rest after the exciting day."

"What does my excitement mean compared to what is going on there?" I answered, pointing at the ghetto.

Like most Poles, Dziuka had no awareness of the Jewish tragedy. The fate of the doomed Jews was of little concern to her or the M family, with the exception of Janusz, who had a few friends in the ghetto.

Nevertheless, during my stay on Kryniczna Street the progress of the Jewish resistance in the ghetto became a daily topic. From the underground press I knew the Germans had entered the ghetto on April 19, but were caught in the cross fire between Mila and Zamenhofa Streets. The next day, the first day of Passover, new German units, reinforced by tanks, were repelled by heavy fire.

Defense post

Guerillas

The Germans withdrew twice but came back with their forces redoubled. Meanwhile, the ghetto fighters had fortified some of the factories as centers of resistance and had taken up guerilla tactics. The Germans, anxious to break the exceptionally strong opposition of the ghetto fighters, resorted to a diabolical plan of setting the entire ghetto ablaze. The incendiary bombs and explosives succeeded in chasing the Jews out of the attics, dug-outs and cellars and caused confusion among the ghetto fighters. Entire blocks were set afire, barring access to strongholds, destroying ammunition and disrupting resistance. The flames were able to accomplish what the arms could not.

Men, women and children were dying by the thousands. There was no escape. The Aryan part of Warsaw was tightly sealed off; and the Poles, threatened with reprisals for harboring Jews, were afraid to take risks. The police were alerted and special police agents combed the streets looking for escapees.

Tipped off by a neighbor, one "secret agent" came to Kryniczna Street looking for "a Jewess who should be burning in the ghetto and was instead among Aryans." Luckily I was not home, and Dziuka denied all knowledge about me. After the man left, she was quite shaken and felt the intrusion was the work of an informer, who might strike again. After an agonizing discussion, it was decided that I must move out again. I was homeless once more, but under happier circumstances because Mira had her own apartment.

During my stay on Kryniczna Street my sister's landlady, disgusted with Mira's visitors, demanded that she vacate the room. At about the same time, Mira heard about a small apartment on Obroncow Street. She promptly contacted the building's superintendent and rented the place.

The house looked like a mansion but was actually divided into apartments. The ground floor, occupied by a middle-aged couple, served as a kind of social meeting place for all tenants. The two upper floors were occupied by two younger couples, both childless, but with dogs and cats.

Mira's apartment was on the first floor near the staircase landing. The smallest in the building, it was awkwardly shaped and had a huge Venetian door leading to a balcony. When I arrived, Mira took me to her quarters, loaded with over-sized furniture, including a double bed, cupboard, table, two chairs and a gas range which served as a kitchen.

Mira seemed happy with her new apartment and her privacy. She was liked by the tenants, who promptly admitted her to their circle. There was no doubt that my untimely arrival could create suspicion among the tenants concerning her identity.

Not to complicate matters, we decided that my presence should be kept secret although this was not easy in small quarters. On the first morning of my stay, an unexpected visit from an upstairs neighbor forced me barefoot into the narrow partition between the closet and the wall, where I shivered for almost an hour.

Late in the afternoon, "Mother" brought a few bulletins about the latest events in the ghetto. I was afraid her visits might lead the "secret agent" to us. So far, he knew only Dziuka; but with assistance from the

154

Doomed in the Ghetto

informer, he was probably able to identify all members of the family. There was no doubt he too was an impostor; but what if he were a member of the same gang of hoodlums who terrorized me before and who might again terrorize the M family in order to reach us?

"Mother" assured me she had taken precautions and had not been followed. She was quite shaken herself after a narrow escape from a trolley car that had been stopped by the Nazis and searched for illegal literature and weapons. The news she brought was disturbing.

The Underground National Army was enthusiastic about the heroism of the Jewish ghetto fighters, but only on paper. There was 155

Hopeless struggle

nothing in the reports to indicate their readiness to assist the Jews in the struggle against the mutual enemy. A similar attitude marked the reports of the Underground People's Army, who responded to the fight with admiration but rendered little material assistance. Their publications reprinted the daily communiqués of the National Jewish Committee, making it apparent that the situation in the ghetto was critical.

For days on end the ghetto was ablaze, and the Jews were burning alive. Nevertheless, the fires did not shatter the determination of the ghetto fighters. In May, organized resistance finally ceased in the ghetto, leaving nests of fighters active until June. When it was over, some survivors reached the Aryan part of Warsaw through the wall and the sewers. A few managed to reach the manholes and escape to the forests. Even there the Nazis succeeded in trailing them with the help of hostile peasants; only those who found refuge in the hide-outs provided by the partisans survived.

The Polish Underground, impressed by the heroic ghetto resistance while it lasted, showed their usual indifference to the few survivors. But the Jewish sacrifice was not in vain. The infallible German might has been broken, giving a new impulse to the Polish freedom fighters, who increased their subversive activities. In order to stop them, the Nazis tightened their grip on the population, still pretending to hunt Jewish escapees from the ghetto.

After the final destruction of the ghetto, the number of Jewish fugitives continued to increase. They tried to contact their political comrades, professional friends, business acquaintances and neighbors, but the number of Poles willing to risk their lives for Jews was exceedingly small. Some Jews found temporary refuge but soon discovered they were prey to greed and blackmail. The number of extortionists grew; they operated all over town, looking for victims to exploit and denounce.

Under these trying conditions, keeping an outside job was dangerous and involved great hazard. Mira was forced to give up her

Escape through sewers

temporary employment and our resources dwindled. Then one of our neighbors hired her and taught her the art of textile weaving. The work was strenuous but we decided to buy our own loom and establish ourselves. I dyed the yarn and handled it on a spinning wheel; Mira did the weaving. The stimulating work gave us tremendous satisfaction and took away the worries from our daily life. Soon we had a group of customers, who recommended us to their friends.

"Mother" was a constant visitor and helped us with the sales. From her bulletins we learned the Germans were losing ground on both the Russian and Allied Fronts. In order to maintain their grasp locally, they kept the population of Warsaw under constant surveillance. Blockades of entire streets set up by the SS, assisted by the police, were the order of the day, with subsequent arrests of all suspects.

One July morning a heavy motorcade moved in and blocked off our street. It was swarming with Polish police, who swiftly cut off both exits and assisted the Germans in a systematic check of houses. We dressed quickly and waited. A bang on the door announced the intruders. Mira ran down the steps and opened the door to a middle-aged, bespectacled German sergeant, who followed her upstairs. He entered our room and without looking at me, approached the loom and examined the fabric. Fascinated by the unusual pattern, which I called "The Flyers," he timidly asked for a swatch. Mira promptly obliged him with an extra-generous sample, and the sergeant left smiling.

After the Germans moved to another block, Mira went to warn the boys on Kryniczna Street. By then it was obvious that the purpose of the blockade was to arrest all young Polish males. All was clear and no one stopped her. When she reached the house, one of the tenants standing outside turned to his wife and commented with irony: "Look at this 'courageous' Jewess!"

Terror was rampant. The nightly street blockades were followed by the execution of suspects during the day. The pacification, enforced by the military, produced an adverse reaction in the Polish Underground, which steadily increased its activity of killing important Germans, among them Franz Kutscher, the notorious "butcher of Warsaw." The Germans followed with reprisals similar to those formerly reserved for Jews.

Until the Warsaw Uprising on August 1, we lived in an atmosphere of excitement, which culminated with the massive German evacuation. The entire population witnessed the movement of German

Sisters

armed forces through the capital. The procession of tanks, trucks, artillery and infantry was miles long. Tired, dirty, and sometimes barefoot Germans begged for water. Several convoys, returning from the Russian front, passed our windows. At noon, one column stopped for a rest. It was the Hermann Goering SS division, which fought in Stalingrad. Although the soldiers were mostly disabled, their very presence under our windows quickened my heartbeat. I could not help but compare these helpless invalids to the arrogant SS "black angels" marching to the Russian front in 1942. What a drastic change.

With the German retreat on the Russian front, the attack on Warsaw gained momentum. Each night Russian air squadrons unloaded thousands of incendiary bombs over the city. The air raids, accompanied by shrill sirens and loud explosions, were music to our ears. They also forced us to seek shelter in the basement where I posed as Mira's cousin. There I met all the tenants, including the Jewish owner of the ground floor apartment who had remained in hiding throughout the war.

One morning, particularly heavy detonations rushed us out of bed. We left our room half-dressed and almost fell down the stairs when a huge explosion shook the entire building. The crash of broken glass suggested a direct hit. The pressure opened the door to the ground floor apartment where some of the tenants had been injured by glass. One of them in danger of losing an eye needed immediate help. I rushed to the nearest phone and called an ambulance. When the injured were picked up, we returned to our room and found that our bed was strewn with debris and broken glass.

In September, the Russians further intensified their attack on the capital and forced the Germans to evacuate the eastern part of the city. Several streets were emptied in Saska Kepa, and the population was moved to the western part of the borough.

During the action I met a few relatives and friends who had remained in hiding—including my sister-in-law Anne and her mother, whom I had last seen in 1939. Our emotional encounter was watched by a policeman who supervised the move. We had a chance to exchange addresses but were separated again when the street was showered by an artillery barrage. My group reached a nearby bomb shelter where we spent the night.

Day after day we were moved from one street to another, from one shelter to the next. Totally exhausted, we made a final effort to return at night to the evacuated part of Saska Kepa, which was out of bounds to civilians. The flat on Kryniczna Street was empty. We closed all the windows and stayed in the darkness in order not to attract the attention of the police, who were watching the streets. Not far from us the German anti-aircraft artillery continued firing. It was difficult staying in the apartment and we moved to the cellar.

Then came September 10. The earth shook under heavy artillery fire, and a fierce air battle was underway. German reflectors combed the sky in fruitless pursuit of the Russian formations, flying at high altitudes. The barrage was so intense that it lit up the darkness and started a number of fires, which turned houses into piles of rubble. In addition, soundless missiles came in waves, forcing us to stay in the shelter.

In the middle of the night, all calmed down for a while. Then the bombing resumed at a considerable distance. Totally exhausted, we dragged ourselves upstairs and fell asleep. At dawn, animated voices came from the outside. I couldn't understand what would bring people to this part of the borough in defiance of the German order. I opened the window and learned that during the night Saska Kepa had been taken by the Russians.

Mira and I looked at each other in disbelief. We tried to seal in our hearts and minds the moment of a return to life. If we only could share this precious moment with our dearest ones, our parents and Bobus—and with the nameless and countless brethren, who suffered, prayed and hoped to survive—but didn't live to see.

162

EPILOGUE

A CONFERENCE DEALING with the growing ferment in Warsaw took place August 10, 1943. The Governor of Warsaw, Ludwig Fischer, presided. Fischer decided to enact a quick pacification plan to begin in October. The preparations for the plan were entrusted to 13,000 civilian agents. The activities of this large body were brought to the attention of the Polish Underground, which hastened to warn its members. Secret information was obtained and a number of reports issued by the Underground. Some are still in existence. One reads: "Report 17.VIII, 1943: Do not keep. Destroy. Under Gestapo surveillance are the houses on Skaryszewska 46; Bracka 16; Gorczewska 6; Hoza 13; Obroncow 16." My sister's apartment was located on Obroncow 16; she lived there in 1943, unaware that the house was being watched by the Gestapo.

We learned from an eyewitness that our parents, Anna and Tewja Krugman, had been killed in Zwierzyniec shortly after we left them on the fatal October 21, 1942. They refused to obey the order of a German who marched them to the collection center. They were buried in a mass grave in Zwierzyniec. Our families in Bialystok were deported in February 1943. My two brothers, Heshel (Escha) and Samuel (Mela), reached Canada via Russia and Japan. Escha joined the Polish units of the Canadian Army and volunteered for paratroop service in Europe. He survived the war and moved with his wife Anne and her mother, Helen Mozelman, to Canada. Mela died from multiple sclerosis during the war.

My husband's parents, Esther and Iser Gurdus, and his sister Genia Kessler with her family perished in the Warsaw Ghetto. His sister Gucia perished in the Riga Ghetto. Leon, Kuba's older brother escaped with his wife Sophie to Mexico. Goslawa, his oldest sister and her husband Abraham Joseph Stybel reached the United States. Nathan, Kuba's younger brother, was evacuated with his wife Irene by the British Embassy and reached Palestine. Another sister, Rosa Igiel, and her family made their way to the United States via Japan. Kuba reached Palestine via Russia. There he volunteered for the Jewish units of the Eighth British Army and served during the entire war. Still in uniform, he came to Warsaw in December 1945, to take us out of Poland.

Kuba's effort to rescue us began in 1942 after an agreement between the Allies and Germany was concluded for the exchange of German prisoners of war for Allied nationals under German occupation. The exchange was earmarked to take place in Istanbul, Turkey, under the auspices of the Swiss Red Cross. Allegedly, an official of the Swiss Red Cross arrived in Zwierzyniec in August 1942. He didn't find us at home, and our neighbors, unaware of his true mission, took him for a Gestapo undercover agent and did not disclose our whereabouts.

Kuba's second attempt at rescue came in 1944 after William Forest, an English war correspondent, saw me in Lublin. He transmitted my message to my brother-in-law Nathan. Thereafter, Kuba secured a special permit to proceed from his unit in Italy to Palestine to submit a request for my visa. His petition was met with little sympathy. When he returned to his unit he decided to try again, this time in writing.

In the meantime the office of the High Commissioner of Palestine passed on to Field Marshal Lord Gort, who was more favorably disposed, and advised my husband that the British Embassy in Moscow had been instructed to find and assist me. The Embassy tried to contact me in Lublin but I had moved to Warsaw. Consequently, this attempt also failed. Nevertheless, the main advantage of this effort was that my file found its way from the British Embassy in Moscow to the British Embassy in Warsaw.

When the British Embassy was established in liberated Warsaw, the British authorities contacted me and assured me that as the wife of a member of H. M. Forces I would be flown to London as soon as RAF services were availalbe to civilians.

In the meantime, my husband decided not to wait any longer and proceeded from Vienna to Warsaw to hasten our reunion. After a dangerous and tedious journey, which required secretly crossing the Russian Zone in Austria and traveling unofficially through Poland, Kuba made his way to Warsaw. When he arrived he immediately proceeded to Hoza 13. We met at the entrance to the building.

Kuba helped to secure Mira's official travel documents, and we left Warsaw in January 1946.

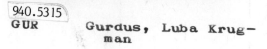
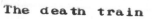

5